RESOURCE ALLOCATION IN BRITISH UNIVERSITIES

RESOURCE ALLOCATION IN BRITISH UNIVERSITIES

Edited by

MICHAEL SHATTOCK & GWYNNETH RIGBY

CUA Resource Allocation Group

SOCIETY FOR RESEARCH INTO HIGHER EDUCATION

The Conference of University Administrators was established in 1973 and exists to encourage the professional development of university administrators.

To achieve this objective the CUA

a provides opportunities for members to meet and exchange ideas mainly through the medium of an annual conference;

b provides a forum for discussion of current problems in tertiary education;

c stimulates training activities, both by the provision of specific training opportunities and by the monitoring of the training programmes and policies of other organizations;

d issues publications from time to time in the furtherance of the objective of the organization;

e facilitates the exchange of information on administrative activities;

f establishes and maintains links with administrators in tertiary education overseas;

g encourages the development of branches in individual institutions to act as a link between members and the central organization of CUA.

At present there are approximately 1,500 members located in some 100 different universities, colleges or institutions within the university system in the United Kingdom and Eire.

Full membership is open to members of staff of United Kingdom universities paid on the national administrative salary structure, to equivalent members of staff of certain other bodies in or allied to the United Kingdom university sector, and to certain other members of staff of universities. Associate membership is open to former members under certain conditions, to overseas university administrators, and to certain other persons.

Initial inquiries should be sent to the chairman, Mr M.A. Higgins, Senior Assistant Registrar, Loughborough University of Technology, Ashby Road, Loughborough, Leicester LE11 3TU.

Research into Higher Education Monographs

The Society for Research into Higher Education, At the University,
Guildford, Surrey GU2 5XH

First published 1983

ISBN 0 900868 97 X

Printed in England by Direct Design (Bournemouth) Ltd. Printers
Butts Pond Industrial Estate, Sturminster Newton,
Dorset DT10 1AZ

FOREWORD

This study was carried out under the auspices of the Conference of University Aministrators. In May 1979 the Conference's Executive Committee established a group with the following terms of reference: To examine the various main approaches adopted by UK universities to the allocation of their resources, to describe and compare some selected examples, to consider their effectiveness within their particular university context and to present a report.

The membership of the group which conducted the study was:

M. L. Shattock, Academic Registrar, University of Warwick (Chairman)

R. Butler, Secretary of Faculties, University of Oxford

S. R. Bosworth, Registrar, University of Salford

R. G. Dobson, Senior Assistant Bursar (Finance), University of Leeds

J. H. Farrant, Senior Assistant Secretary, University of Sussex

J. H. Ford, Finance Officer, University of Essex

M. D. Forster, Registrar, University of Lancaster

P. H. Gayward, Finance Officer, University of Liverpool

J. E. Glasspool, Secretary, School of Management, Cranfield Institute of Technology

B. B. Mayes, Buildings Officer, University of Sheffield

R. A. Newstead, Finance Officer, University of East Anglia

J. T. Suddaby, Assistant Secretary, University of Edinburgh

Dr. B. J. R. Taylor, Planning Officer, University of Bath

A. D. Weir, Finance Officer, University of Glasgow

Ms. F. G. Rigby, Senior Assistant Registrar, University of Warwick (Secretary)

The Group held its first meeting in November 1979 and thereafter met regularly either as a full group or as various sub-sets for discussion of particular topics up to July 1982. As part of its inquiries it made a series of visits to universities to study their resource allocation processes: Cranfield Institute of Technology, East Anglia, Edinburgh, Salford, Sheffield and Warwick. These were a very valuable part of the study and we wish to express our gratitude to the universities concerned both for their hospitality and for the time and trouble which was taken by their staffs, both academic and administrative, to answer our many questions. In addition we derived considerable benefit from a visit to the Secretary and other officers of the University Grants Committee (UGC). The majority of our meetings were held in the University of London Senate House and we wish to record our thanks to Gordon Chubb for making such excellent arrangements for us.

The Group sought to obtain an international perspective on resource allocation problems in higher education. Three members (Taylor, Shattock and Suddaby) attended the Fifth General Conference of the Institutional Management in Higher Education Programme held under OECD auspices in Paris in September 1980 and a paper deriving from that conference, 'University resource allocation procedures: responses to change' (Shattock), was subsequently published in the *International Journal of IMHE* Vol. 5, No. 3 in November 1981. Two members (Farrant and Taylor) also attended the Annual Conference of the International Association for Institutional Research in November 1980 and a paper deriving from that conference, 'Resource allocation in UK universities' (Taylor), was published in the *AIR Professional File* No. 11, Spring 1982. Taylor also published a paper for CUA entitled 'Norms and formulae in resource allocation' (CUA Occasional Paper No. 3, 1981).

The Group obtained a grant of $52,000 from the Exxon Education Foundation, with assistance from the Ford Foundation and the Lilly Endowment, to hold a two-day conference in New York in August 1981 to make a comparative study of British and American approaches to university resource allocation. Thirty-five senior US academics and administrators with interests and responsibilities in this field accepted the Group's invitation to attend. The grant also enabled the Group to invite the Secretary General and Executive Secretary of the Committee of Vice-Chancellors and Principals (CVCP) (G.K. Caston and B.H. Taylor) and a member of the secretariat of the UGC (J. Walne) to attend. We wish to express our appreciation to our American and British colleagues for their contributions and our gratitude in particular to Dr. Robert A. Scott (Director of Academic Affairs, Indiana State Commission for Higher Education) who jointly chaired the conference, to Steve D. Campbell and the good offices of the National Association of College and University Business Officers (NACUBO) for its administrative support, to Dr. George D. Sussman and the New York State Education Department for hosting an extended visit by the Group to talk to university, campus and state officials in Albany, and most of all to Dr. Richard R. Johnson, Director of Research at the Exxon Foundation, for his constant support and encouragement.

The study was assisted by discussions with university colleagues up and down the country and by the comments of participants at three annual CUA conferences. We are particularly grateful to our own universities for support during a long, intensive and, for us, rewarding inquiry.

CONTENTS

TABLES AND FIGURES

TABLES

FIGURES

Tables and Figures

INTRODUCTION

Resource allocation has always been a subject of intense interest within universities, but the cuts imposed on university expenditure in 1981 have given it an added public interest. The high cost of university teaching and research and the limitation on funds made available from public sources inevitably leads to intense competition for resources at every level: at the national level between the university system and the public sector of higher education; at the system level, between institutions seeking resources from the UGC; and at the institutional level between the various academic, administrative and other interests represented within universities. This study is primarily concerned with resource allocation at the institutional level, but because decisions at the institutional level are dependent on UGC and government resource allocation procedures we have also sought to describe how the various processes fit together.

Our detailed inquiries were concentrated on a limited number of institutions which seemed to us to be broadly representative of the British university system outside Oxbridge and London, where the collegiate structure creates a special situation. But our knowledge of the university system extended more widely than this and examples are drawn from a larger spectrum of institutions. We have deliberately chosen, however, not to identify institutions. Primarily this reflects the basis on which we sought information from universities but it also serves to emphasize that our concern is to describe institutional models of resource allocation rather than how a particular university allocates its resources. Throughout the text, therefore, institutions are indicated by letters A, B, C, etc., and to avoid a simple identification from the figures quoted no one letter is consistently applied to a single institution. By the same token, we have not been concerned to comment on the detailed priorities adopted in resource allocation in individual institutions. The strength of the British universities is in part derived from their diversity of approach to resource allocation which their (relative) autonomy, as conferred through the 'block grant' system, gives them. In the circumstances we did not feel that comment on the results of the resource allocation process in particular universities would be helpful or justified, though we have commented on the various approaches we examined and on the criteria used.

Our inquiries also included the Cranfield Institute of Technology, a university institution which does not come under the UGC or have membership of the CVCP. Where comparisons are made with Cranfield it is, however, identified, since its processes and procedures are not at all typical of other institutions in the public sector of higher education.

The way an institution allocates its resources says a great deal about how it views its priorities consciously and unconsciously. We have not, therefore, limited our study solely to the allocation of money derived from the UGC, but have sought to include the total financial resources available to universities together with those capital resources which can reasonably be described as being available for allocation on an annual or regular basis: in practice, this means academic accommodation, and the equipment and furniture grant. We were concerned to describe how institutions allocated their resources, and what were their different styles, methods, techniques and decision-making structures.

It is often not appreciated outside a university, or even amongst university staff not directly concerned in the process, that the annual internal resource allocation process constitutes a continuous and, to some individuals and officers within a university, a dominant sub-plot to the course of each academic year. The process extends throughout the year, beginning in most institutions with the collection of data, financial and statistical, from the previous years' operations, and continuing through a cycle of meetings to final decisions on which the academic programmes for the following year will need to be based. The process takes place at multiple levels, at Council and Senate, at Faculty or School meetings, and in particular at committees or sub-committees of these bodies, as well as at the department or subject unit levels. It is important to note that this study covers only the central decision-making process, that is the mechanism for resource allocation at Council and Senate levels, and only takes in the Faculty or School level in so far as it serves as an adjunct to Senate machinery. The study does not seek to examine the mechanisms employed at the primary spending unit level, whether this is at the departmental or subject level, or at the Faculty level, in universities where budgetary control is devolved to Faculty spending groups.

It is difficult to discuss resource allocation processes without using terms like 'effectiveness', 'efficiency' or 'equity' which import value judgements about the end purpose of the exercise. Resource allocation is not an end in itself but a means of fulfilling institutional objectives. These objectives may have been decided as part of a forward planning process or may be implicit in the structure of the institution: they may have been formally agreed or they may represent an overt understanding within the institution. In some institutions, however, there is no agreement, or no mechanism for reaching agreement, on planning objectives or priorities. In such cases the resource allocation process defines the objectives as they exist at the time the relevant allocation decisions are taken and these, as a consequence, may be internally inconsistent and reflect the lack of a co-ordinated approach.

'Effectiveness' therefore must be a measure of the extent to which the resource allocation process fulfils planning objectives and priorities. 'Efficiency' on the other hand measures how the process works, how much time it consumes, whether it is cost-effective, whether it commands institutional confidence, whether it is internally consistent. The concept of 'equity' is harder to define. In this study equity does not mean, as it is sometimes taken to mean, equal shares for all, or equality of misery, but whether the process provides an opportunity for a full assessment of all the known factors and views expressed so as to permit a balanced judgement to take place. An effective, efficient and equitable resource allocation system will not guarantee an institution's academic success but it should provide conditions within an institution which will foster it.

Resource allocation and forward planning in higher education are often discussed as if they constitute a single process. In fact many universities have separate, if linked, processes. In theory, once an academic plan is made the resource allocation process naturally follows the plans and priorities agreed. In practice, because of the way universities receive their funds, and in particular because of the timing of the announcement of the funding levels, their planning and resource allocation have in the last decade rarely gone hand in hand. The bureaucratic uncertainties and obscurities of the Department of Education and Science (DES)/UGC funding mechanism, the sharp changes of direction by the Government, virtually the sole paymaster of the universities, and the fluctuations of inflation, student demand, and social pressures, have meant that planning and resource allocation processes have become increasingly uncoupled over the years; although in the post-July 1981 situation they may be moving closer together again. We believe that the resource allocation process has a sufficiently discrete identity to merit a study on its own, and that it has enabled us to shed light on how universities exercise their self-governing powers, and on the ways they have adapted to the pressures of cuts in resources. We hope it will be useful to universities and their staffs in re-examining the exercise of what is their most important administrative responsibility.

It is in fact surprising that resource allocation in British universities has not previously attracted a large-scale examination. In part this probably reflects a disinclination in Britain, in contrast to the United States, to regard higher education as a serious subject of study in spite of its general public importance. Partly it may also be because the actual processes of resource allocation can be highly technical and are difficult to understand and communicate to a wider audience. Perhaps another reason is that both the internal and external processes of university resource allocation have changed very rapidly in the last two decades and a snap shot view at any given moment would have been unlikely to provide any kind of comprehensive or stable picture of what was actually going on. It would be unreasonably optimistic to hope that the pace of change in the future will be slower than in the past: we have therefore sought to describe the system now, even in its current state of flux. We have received regular reminders, however, during the course of the study, of the difficulty of describing a constantly moving target.

In the early 1960s there were many universities which still operated under a system where effectively the Vice-Chancellor, acting alone, decided on the allocation of resources in detail, academic department by department. In an extreme case one university had no formal process at all, resources being allocated for academic purposes on ad hoc demand to the Secretary of the university who personally decided and later reported on the matter to the university's governing body. Such procedures often excited adverse comment within institutions but the fundamental reason why they became unworkable and were gradually abandoned was the growing size of institutional budgets and the growing diversity and complexity of the institutions themselves. Of course the process of democratization or, more properly described, of increased participation in university government, assisted the changeover to a more formal and open decision-making structure, but essentially the pressure came from the need to match the student and budgetary growth targets laid down by the UGC, within its highly structured and systematized quinquennial planning and budgeting period, with a complementary internal planning and resource allocation process. The first serious account of the resource allocation process, by John Fielden and Geoffrey Lockwood in 1973,[1] assumed 'that the resource allocation exercises are undertaken against a background of agreed priorities stated in a quinquennial submission (ie to the UGC) and rephrased annually in a set of planning assumptions.'[2] Fielden in an earlier report (1969)[3] found a growing use of formulae in forward planning but compared the British systematization of planning unfavourably with the situation in the US, where 81% of state universities responding to Rourke and Brook's survey used some kind of formulae in their budget preparation.

By 1973 the use of norms and formulae in British universities had, according to Fielden and Lockwood, become extensive, but this brought with it the danger that decisions would be made mechanically on historic data. 'The equity principle,' they wrote, 'as a basis for resource allocation is rooted deep and is seen in such actions as extrapolations *pro rata* of student numbers in departments to a given university target at the end of the quinquennium or a percentage cut-back for all on departmental consumable budgets. Such conclusions are easier than selective and priority ranking exercises and they have a comforting psychological effect in that all feel that even if justice has not been done, no-one will have suffered unduly.'[5] They concluded that most planning was 'additive' in character and 'dominated by the aim to achieve an equitable distribution of resources'. There were few examples of 'a university creating room for development by eliminating or reducing existing commitments.'[6]

A second account of resource allocation processes was published in 1974 by Graeme Moodie and Rowland Eustace.[7] Their account was concerned much more with the political side of the process. They suggested that 'the move towards a more numerate, analytic and systematic base for decision making may produce a corresponding shift of political influence into the hands of the officials most intimately involved in preparing that base.'[8] They described the creation of central planning committees which assessed each claim by reference to university priorities and criteria and then made recommendations to Senate or Council. They stressed, as did Fielden and Lockwood, the need for a comprehensive management information system so that the most relevant data could be brought together to assist resource allocation decisions. Although they admitted that 'hunch and struggle can never entirely be eliminated from any process of government' they nevertheless expected that the processes they described would reinforce rationality in decision-taking and 'substitute informed judgement for mere guess work.'[9] Both accounts quoted so far were profoundly influenced by the relative optimism of the 1967-72 quinquennium, which coincided with an increasing awareness in universities of the virtues of long-range planning and the use of quantitative techniques. The 1972 White Paper *Education: A Framework for Expansion*,[10] while disappointing to some in its forecasts of the rate of expansion in student numbers up to 1981-82 by comparison with the projections published in 1970 in DES Planning Paper No. 2,[11] nevertheless emphasized the importance of accepting a lengthy timescale for educational planning.

A more pessimistic description of university resource allocation was published by Tony Becher and Maurice Kogan in 1980.[12] They distinguish three approaches to resource allocation: oligarchic, bureaucratic and collegial. The oligarchic describes the autocratic institutional head which they believe still exists in a few institutions or the allocation based on 'a contest between robber barons' where the beneficiaries of the budget carve it up between them, usually through a committee on which all the heads of the 'basic units' sit.[13] The bureaucratic approach is to hide 'budgetary problems under a cloak of arithmetic impartiality', thus eliminating academic discussion by automatic allocations based on norms and formulae.[14] The collegial approach involves widespread circulation and acceptance of relevant information, the creation of 'a small tribunal of reasonably independent academics' and the establishment of an appeals procedure.[15] All three forms they admit suffer from disadvantages, and none of them is particularly effective in adapting to a situation of retrenchment. Their conclusions represent a far cry from the optimism of their predecessors. They underline what they see as the weakness of the 'peer group principle' when applied to institutional resource allocation. 'Academics,' they say, 'though conscientious in framing judgements within their own areas of expertise, show little commitment to making sound decisions about the issues which affect the running of their own institutions.'[16]

These accounts constitute probably the best general statement about resource allocation in British universities. But they provide an over-simplified view. Perhaps the most striking feature we have found is the lack of homogeneity in the resource allocation processes of different universities. In a university system which has one of the most centralized processes for resource allocation at the national level of any of the major industrialized nations, the institutions themselves have retained a remarkable degree of constitutional and procedural diversity. It is clear that there is no right or best package of processes and procedures. The single most essential feature is that institutions have confidence in them. In the July 1981 UGC allocation for the 1981-82 to 1983-84 period, two of the universities which appeared to have been most favourably treated were at opposite ends of what for a convenient shorthand one might call the managerial and the participative approaches to resource allocation. One university allocated all its resources through a Vice-Chancellor's advisory committee which appeared to do no more than report to the Senate, while the other allocated its academic resources through a Senate committee, not chaired by the Vice-Chancellor, which was elected by the Senate and had a built-in appeals committee structure. It could be argued that processes and procedures are less important and should not be confused with the assumptions and data on which institutions actually take their decisions. But even here there are wide dissimilarities between, for example, institutions that use national averages as guides to staff/student ratios and departmental expenses and institutions which have devised norms and formulae of their own to assist the allocation process. Nevertheless, as might be expected from the pervasive homogeneity of the UGC's assumptions and criteria, there is less variation in the basic assumptions which lie behind decision-making at the institutional level than might be suggested by the differences in procedures which lead up to it.

The difficulty is to assess how far differences in process and procedure actually affect the allocations made. Does a system which provides for an allocation to be made to the university library before any other academic area in the university have the effect of skewing resources towards the library? Does the lack of co-ordination implied by a system in which departmental expenses are allocated by the finance committee of Council whilst the funds for academic and non-academic posts are decided upon by different committees of Senate lead to a balance of allocation for the academic programme of the university different from that where all such allocations are handled by one committee only? Where one committee allocates all university resources, academic and administrative, is the balance of allocation for, say, maintenance of premises or administrative services different from that where such allocations are made entirely separately?

What has become impressed upon us is the extent to which universities have developed very distinct institutional styles. Partly, and some would say very largely, this relates to their history and origins. The older civic universities have developed their systems over a lengthy period of years. To the outsider they sometimes look muddled and inefficient, but the insiders know the conventions, and systems that otherwise look unmanageable seem to work adequately because they are held together by a sense of corporate understanding. Such systems seem, however, to be resistant to change. The technological universities with their former college of advanced technology background seem generally to follow a more top-down approach than elsewhere, perhaps reflecting the position of the principal or director under the former LEA control. The new foundations, on the other hand, tend to be more 'collegial' in style, to use Becher and Kogan's phrase, than the rest. None of these generalizations, however, is wholly accurate. There are institutional exceptions, and exceptions within universities in relation to particular areas of the budget.

There is no question but that external pressures have played an important role in forming the internal university processes and procedures for resource allocation. The changeover from resource alloction by a Vice-Chancellor, either on his own or through his Council's finance committee, to the more elaborate planning committee structure, which drew its legitimacy from the implementation and phasing of the quinquennial plan, has been described above with reference to Fielden and Lockwood. The salient point is that prior to the period of university expansion, resource allocation was a relatively unadulterated process. The university had financial resources and each year divided them up amongst the various heads of estimate, while attempting to retain an adequate reserve. In the period of expansion, however, UGC resources were linked to student numbers, with norms dictating different allocations for different subject fields. Internal resource allocation became to a large extent subordinate to student number targets. Once the quinquennial plan had been adopted with student numbers attached to particular developments, it was incumbent upon the institution to allocate its resources broadly according to those numbers. Of course it was not as simple as that because subject areas fluctuated in popularity amongst university entrants so that many universities compensated in their planning and resource allocation for student number shortfalls in the physical sciences and engineering with accelerated growth in arts and social studies. Nevertheless student numbers were the counters crucial to the game rather than finance as such. Very few universities chose to restrict growth in the popular fields of study to stay in balance with the less popular, if it meant handing back or, in practice, not bidding for resources expected to be available from the UGC.

This approach to resource allocation tended to persist in spite of the breakdown of the quinquennial system in the mid-1970s, because student numbers continued to expand broadly in line with UGC target numbers. A warning shot was fired from Cambridge in a report in 1975[17] which recommended bringing expansion at Cambridge 'to a close in an orderly manner whilst developing the necessary procedures for coping with a steady state.'[18] The report recognized that 'as long as a university is growing it can change the balance of its activities by channelling new money into growing areas without actually cutting back the resources given to declining ones.'[19]

But the central problem facing the steady state university was the need 'to devise means of changing the balance of teaching and research activities within a budget which remains virtually constant in real terms.' [20]

This report seemed prophetic for the university system as a whole when in 1979 the Government declared a policy of 'level funding' towards higher education.[21] When the Government admitted that the system was now 'expenditure led'[22] and that student numbers were no longer the determinant of policy, planning and resource allocation at the UGC level were immediately affected and the impact soon made itself felt on the processes and procedures of resource allocation within institutions. The detail of how retrenchment affected the planning and resource allocation structures which universities had laboriously created for themselves is described in subsequent chapters. It is only necessary to note here that the period 1979-82 has seen very considerable changes. Well tried participative machinery was found in some universities not to be satisfactory and smaller bodies composed of appointed rather than elected members effectively took over some of its functions. Extended decision-making systems tended to be concertina-ed to speed up decisions. Resources rather than student numbers became the dominant feature. These dramatic changes, however, did not necessarily lead to the abandonment of the formal constitutional processes and procedures which had grown up to deal with an expansion of student numbers. Two conflicting systems often continued, the new imposed on the old. In other universities, reforms conceived after the first impact of 'level funding' had to be put aside to cope with the further crisis occasioned by the UGC's financial settlement for the 1981-2 to 1983-4 period. In many universities procedures are in a state of flux.

The Resource Allocation Group came together in late 1979. It began its work by examining the systems of resource allocation which universities curently had in place. These on the whole reflected the structures based on the processes of the early 1970s. But as we proceeded, the rules of the game at DES and UGC level changed very rapidly and university structures changed with them so that our account of resource allocation procedures, rather than being a description of a settled, if developing, system, became an account of how universities are adjusting their processes and procedures to very rapid changes in resource levels, as well as a description of the structures from which these changes are emerging.

Perhaps the most valuable part of our study was actually carried out in visits to universities. Our experience, based very much on interviews conducted on the visits, would not support Becher and Kogan's conclusion, quoted above, that academics 'show little commitment to making sound decisions about the issues which affect the running of their own institutions.' Certainly the decisions now required are less easy to reach in the kind of committees universities have become used to over the last decade, and institutions have varied very greatly in their ability to cope with the new situation. The strains and stresses of the past three years have put pressure on the 'peer group' system — we discovered in the council chamber of one university a note, presumably passed from one disgruntled member of a resource allocating committee to another: 'Resources seem to move towards pro-vice-chancellors!' — but some universities have proved themselves to be resilient in the present climate without changing their processes and procedures to any significant extent, so it cannot be assumed that the constitutional structures established in the period of expansion are necessarily unable to cope with a period of contraction.

NOTES AND REFERENCES

1 Fielden, J. and Lockwood, G. (1973) *Planning and Management in Universities* Sussex University Press and Chatto and Windus
2 Fielden and Lockwood op.cit. p.221
3 Fielden, J. (1969) *University Management Accounting* University of London
4 Fielden op.cit. p.45
5 Fielden and Lockwood op.cit. p.223
6 Fielden and Lockwood op.cit. p.110
7 Moodie, G.C. and Eustace, R.B. (1974) *Power and Authority in British Universities* George Allen and Unwin
8 Moodie and Eustace op.cit. p.188
9 Moodie and Eustace op.cit. p.194
10 *Education: A Framework for Expansion* (1972) Cmnd 5174. HMSO
11 *Student Numbers in Higher Education in England and Wales* (1970) Education and Planning Paper No.2. HMSO
12 Becher, T. and Kogan, M. (1980) *Process and Structure in Higher Education* Heinemann
13 Becher and Kogan op.cit. p.173
14 Becher and Kogan op.cit. p.174
15 Becher and Kogan op.cit. p.174
16 Becher and Kogan op.cit. p.178
17 *Report of the General Board on the Long Term Development of the University* (1974) Cambridge University Report No. 4884
18 Report of the General Board op.cit. para 44
19 Report of the General Board op.cit. para 49
20 Report of the General Board op.cit. para 49
21 *Government Observations on the First Report from the Education Science and Arts Committee* (1980) Cmnd 8011. HMSO
22 DES Letter to Select Committee on Education, Science and Arts, 3 March 1980. This was the first occasion when the phrase was used to define the new policy.

THE CHANGING FINANCIAL
CONTEXT OF UNIVERSITY RESOURCE ALLOCATION

It is tempting in the context of the reduced resources for the years 1981-82 to 1983-84 to portray the years 1965-1979 as some kind of halcyon period when planning and therefore resource allocation could take place in a settled environment. To understand the resource allocation structures current in 1979, however, it is important to recognize that the financial and political context in which resource allocation had been taking place had been changing and for the most part worsening over the previous decade. With hindsight it is possible to discern a downward trend but at the time there was a tendency, as with the British economy as a whole, to see each step as only a temporary setback, an interruption of a process of improvement and growth which began at around the time of Robbins. One result of this was that university procedures adapted perhaps less quickly to the changing conditions than would otherwise have been the case.

In 1967 Harold Wilson was able to tell the Labour Party Conference at Scarborough that the Government was spending 88% more on higher education than four years previously and that the 1967-72 quinquennial settlement provided for a 10% increase in student unit costs.[1] This represented the high-water mark of university funding post-Robbins. By 1972 the scaling down exercise had begun. In 1970 the UGC had suggested to universities a 'working hypothesis' of 316,000 students in universities by 1976-77, but in December 1972 the White Paper *Education: A Framework for Expansion* had reduced the target to 306,000 and the recurrent allocation to universities included an 'economy factor' of 2% per student.[2] An important feature of this period was that student number targets, and the forward planning and the resource allocation that followed from them, were more dependent on the provision of capital grants for new buildings than on recurrent grant. Academic and residential accommodation represented an expansion bottleneck for many universities. The White Paper's target of 375,000 students in universities by 1981-82 was therefore heavily dependent on a large capital programme. The period 1973 to 1974 was occupied by two fruitless long-range planning exercises for student growth up to 1981-82, one geared to the White Paper figure and the second to a reduced figure of 320,000. Fruitless they may have been but they maintained an impetus for expansion which exercised a fatal attraction in some universities where, as events subsequently showed, a process of consolidation might have been more sensible. First, the Barber moratorium on all capital projects announced in mid-1973, followed by what the UGC described as 'a much reduced building programme for 1975-76', effectively ruled out the achievement of the planned 1981-82 targets.[3] But, more seriously, in January 1974 the Government announced that it was not willing to supplement the 1973-74 recurrent grant for inflation, then running at 12.8% for university costs, and was only willing to contribute 50% of inflation costs for 1974-75. The UGC warned that universities had 'to be prepared for further economies in future years'[4] and the CVCP talked about a 'cash flow crisis' and advised the Government that even if universities could declare staff redundant they could not cover the redundancy costs.

The crisis deepened through 1974 as the Index of University Costs rose by 29.4%. Despite supplementation the recurrent grant for 1974-75 fell short of its planned value by 8.2%. A further cut in the building programme was followed in July by the breakdown of the quinquennial system and a recalculation of targets and grants for 1975-76 and 1976-77. The UGC advised universities that 'You may well think that the overriding restraint may not be the student application rate but the availability of recurrent resources,'[5] and one Vice-Chancellor publicly suggested that it might actually be UGC policy to produce one or two university bankruptcies. This, as it turned out, was a reflection of the pressures of the situation rather than of what was actually happening, and in the following year, 1975-76, the position eased somewhat as a result of the new 'cash limits' policy introduced by the Government in 1975. With the collapse of the quinquennial funding arrangements, and the absence of fully guaranteed supplementation for inflation, the UGC were in a position of considerable uncertainty. In 1974-75 a number of ad hoc measures had been resorted to in order to replace automatic supplementation. Allocations were made from UGC reserves, from unallocated reserves of equipment and furniture grant, from a reduction of the equipment and furniture grant and from two special government allocations made during the year. This hand-to-mouth situation improved in 1975-76, however, because although there was no return to longer range funding the cash limits policy at least gave universities the assurance that the inflation level of the previous year would be written into the grant for the next. In 1975-76 inflation fell below 1974-75 levels and universities therefore benefited to the extent of what the UGC called 'a minimal increase' in resources.

This improvement was, however, somewhat offset within universities by the results of the high inflation of the previous year: a recalculation of student targets, a rent freeze and the creation of a salary anomaly in respect of academic staff in the public sector. In practice perhaps the most serious consequence of the breakdown of the quinquennial system for the internal management of universities lay in the uncertainty created by the timing of grant announcements for the annual financial settlement. When in December 1974 the Government announced an additional grant for 1974-75, it stated that the grant for 1975-76 and 1976-77 would be announced shortly. In March 1975, however, it was only able to announce the 1975-76 grant so that the UGC was only able to complete its distribution in May. In March the UGC passed on a DES expectation that the 1976-77 grant would be announced in late 1975, but it was not announced until March 1976, with a UGC distribution once again in May and a further distribution in September. This began to set a pattern of government announcements in March and UGC distributions in May/June, leaving very little of the academic year left for universiites' own internal allocation of resources, and no opportunity to gear student intakes to recurrent grant fluctuations in the same year. Moreover, a further problem was created by the cash limits policy, because the grant reflected the inflation level of the previous year. If inflation rose in the following year the grant was in theory supplemented. In practice, whether or not inflation had risen could only be determined late in the Government's financial year (April to March), so that each year the UGC and subsequently the universities began to receive inflation supplements for the university financial year (August to July) towards the end of the year in question. The effect of this was that the year began in an atmosphere of grave austerity and ended with a UGC hand-out which sometimes made a mockery of past economy decisions. Psychologically this was distinctly unhelpful to the establishment of a satisfactory environment within universities where planning and resource allocation could go hand in hand. Moreover, large cash sums arriving late in the year were difficult to anticipate and plan for and difficult to allocate to best effect. If placed in a reserve fund they were in danger of fuelling a government complaint that universities held too much in their reserves. It was undoubtedly an inefficient method of university funding, it discouraged rational planning and encouraged ad hocery.

By 1978 the relative success of the Government's pay policy, the settlement of the academic pay anomaly and the resumption of forward planning in the DES with the publication of *Higher Education into the 1990s*[6] suggested a period of greater stability, though the option of a financial 'tunnelling through the hump' of student numbers anticipated over the 1978-1985 period came to have a painful ring to it after July 1981. The change of government in 1979 brought a sharp change of policy. The immediate raising of overseas students fees to 'full cost' levels and the consequent withdrawal of £100m from UGC funding (equivalent to about 12% of the grant) brought an element of uncertainty into university budgeting not experienced even in the worst days of the 1973-74 crisis. The Secretary of State announced a policy of 'level funding', a phrase that was intended 'as a guide to universities to indicate that for planning purposes they should work on the basis that the grant for home students for the academic years 1981-82 and 1982-83 would not be very different in real terms from that announced for 1980-81.'[7] This would have been more convincing if the average student unit cost had not declined by about 13% in real terms between 1974 and 1980. Less than a year later the Secretary of State imposed a further 8½% cut on the university system by 1983-84. At the same time the indexing of university costs gave way to a new cash planning policy.

In October 1980 the chairman of the UGC spelt out the position to the CVCP:

'there is going to be in the future a somewhat greater degree of direct intervention by the UGC in the affairs of individual universities than has been customary or necessary in the past. ... The Committee is quite as staunch a defender of university autonomy as you are. ...

'The fact remains, however, that the reconciling of what is desired *locally* with what is desirable *nationally* can be done almost entirely covertly in an expanding system, where all the signs are positive, and the Committee maintains steerage by selective addition, but in a system where some of the signs are going to be negative, where resources are going to be taken away as well as added, steerage necessarily becomes more overt.

'Of course most of the adding and subtracting is going to be done *internally* by universities without any involvement by the UGC, but there are going to be areas where *change*, some of it unpalatable to particular groups of staff, is going to have to be a collaborative exercise between us — and I mean collaborative — we have always tried to have the fullest consultation with institutions before taking action which will affect them.'[8]

In May 1981, after 'the level funding' guarantee had been withdrawn, in a letter entitled 'The future pattern of resources for universities', the UGC wrote to all universities as follows:

'the orderly development of the system is now threatened by rapid reductions in resources of such magnitude that the Committee's legitimate role and duty to offer guidance to universities based on its acquired knowledge of the system as a whole now assumes a new importance. In particular at a time of rapid change and increased sophistication in some subject areas, the Committee has to try to enable universities to retain scope for new developments and to maintain an adequate "floor" for research. ...'

The UGC made it clear that university expenditure had fallen by 11% as compared with 1979-80. It went on to say:

'It is not the Committee's intention to distribute the cut in resources equally between institutions and fields of study. We have decided that, in order to maintain the vitality and responsiveness of universities, resources must continue to be made available for necessary new developments, as well as for new appointments in fields of special importance. The Committee believes that this can and should be achieved without the closure of any whole university. Regrettably, however, savings

of the order required must involve reducing the range of subjects taught
at some universities, and this will involve recommendations for the
closure or radical reduction of some departments with the likelihood
of consequent redundancies of staff, both academic and non-academic.
There will also be implications for the continued ability to conduct
postgraduate teaching and research in some areas of study in some
institutions.'[9]

On 1 July 1981 the UGC issued its conclusive letter on the so-called
restructuring of the university system:

'In its deliberations the Committee has had to weigh many competing
claims for the diminished resources; for example between subjects,
between institutions, between teaching and research, between innovation
and the continuance of existing areas of work, between provision of
student places and likely demand, and between student numbers and
quality of education. There is of course no single definitive solution to
these problems, partly because the rate at which resources are being
removed from the university system necessarily leads to disorder and
diseconomy whatever path of change is followed, and partly because
reductions in resources are being imposed at a time when demand for
university education is still rising. ...

'Any estimate of the overall loss of recurrent resources between
1979/80 and 1983/84 is subject to numerous uncertainties but it probably
will lie in the range 11% (a minimum estimate by the UGC) and
15% (as suggested by the CVCP). It is the Committee's view that the
university system as a whole should not be asked, with this reduction
in funding, to maintain its home and European Community (EC) student
numbers at the 1979/80 levels, and a reduction of about 5% is therefore
assumed, although this may not be achieved until 1984/85. The
reduction in student numbers by 1983/84 is expected to be in the range
3 to 5%. As to the unit of resource, it will be seen that the Committee
envisages an average worsening of about 10% (including some decline at
all universities) and this figure should be borne in mind when considering
the Committee's guidance below on individual subject areas.'[10]

Later in the same month the chairman of the UGC admitted that the
rate of grant reduction would produce 'friction and inefficiency' and
considerable diseconomies, and that unless non-recurrent grants could be
made to cover redundancy costs several universities would move into
bankruptcy by late 1982-83.[11] In November Sir Keith Joseph, the new
Secretary of State, said that while he deplored unplanned bankruptcies, if
the UGC were to recommend university closures the Government would
listen to its advice.[12]

The period 1972 to 1979 was a time of growing austerity for the university system. The financial crisis for universities in 1974-75 and the recovery thereafter, and particularly the tendency for the UGC to allocate inflation supplements late in the academic year, concealed the underlying trend of government expenditure which was increasingly to give lower priority to higher education. If anything, universities were optimistic in 1979 that a new government would restore the priorities of 1972, especially in view of the Prime Minister's personal role in the 1972 White Paper. University resource allocation structures were therefore in almost all cases geared to a pre-1974-75 situation.

With the benefit of hindsight the UGC and the universities should have paid more attention to the events and public statements of the 1974-75 crisis. Many universities set up wide-ranging economy committees to find ways of reducing expenditure, particularly in managerial areas like maintenance, telephones and other services. In one university the Vice-Chancellor went to the length of inviting all staff and students to send him ideas for economies 'which will be considered in complete confidence by the (economy) committee',[13] a move which excited some understandable apprehension among his academic colleagues. But only one university of the number we have studied fundamentally amended its planning and resource allocation structure as a result of the crisis. In retrospect the pressures of 1974-75 look rather like a profound warning to the universities which the universities did not heed. The resource position has now changed very markedly. Retrenchment and reallocation of resources are the order of the day and as a consequence resource allocation in the 1980s may show marked differences in style and procedure from the 1970s.

NOTES AND REFERENCES

1   Wilson, H. (1974) *The Labour Government 1964-70* p.555. Penguin
2   *Education: A Framework for Expansion* (1972) Cmnd 5174. HMSO
3   UGC letter to universities 'Building programmes' 20 December 1973
4   UGC letter to universities, 18 January 1974
5   UGC letter to universities, 8 July 1974
6   *Higher Education into the 1990s* (1978) A Discussion Document, DES/SED
7   *Government Observations on the First Report from the Education Science and Arts Committee* (1980) Cmnd 8011, para 7. HMSO
8   Address by the Chairman of the UGC to the CVCP, 24 October 1980
9   UGC letter to universities 'The future pattern of resources for universities' 15 May 1981
10 UGC letter to universities 'Grant for 1981-2 and Guidance for succeeding years' 1 July 1981
11 Minutes of Evidence, Select Committee on Education, Science and Arts, 24 July 1981
12 Minutes of Evidence, Select Committee on Education, Science and Arts, 11 November 1981
13 Reported in *University of Leicester Bulletin* (1974) 8 (2) 9

RESOURCE ALLOCATION WITHIN GOVERNMENT AND UGC

It is only too easy to regard university resource allocation as an enclosed process, unconnected with the external world. Events since 1 July 1981 have done a good deal to emphasize the relationship between government policies, UGC priorities and university finances, but the extent to which the university decision-making process reflects resource allocation decisions taken in the Treasury, in the DES and in the UGC is often obscured. The constraints which universities face in resource allocation are mirrored at each level in the decision-making chain. Universities may be autonomous self-governing corporations but in budgetary terms they are firmly tied to a comprehensive system of government resource allocation and expenditure control. Nowhere is this more apparent than in the timetable universities have to adopt for the distribution of the resources available to them. Like all other bodies dependent on Government for support, the universities are inextricably bound by the timing of the Public Expenditure Survey Committee review. PESC was created in 1961 as a means of establishing a longer-term view of the implications of government expenditure than the previous annual estimates of expenditure. The Committee, which is made up of civil servants — departmental finance officers and Treasury staff chaired by a Treasury official — projects the costs of current policies for a five-year period. The PESC cycle begins in November or December with the Treasury sending to departments a statement about the economic assumptions on which they should prepare their spending forecasts for the next five years. Preliminary returns are made by February. Between March and May discussions take place on a bilateral basis between the Treasury and the spending departments and in May PESC meets to agree and issue a report which costs current policies and details areas of disagreement.

The PESC report, which is confidential, then goes to the Chancellor who reports to the Cabinet on how far the total of public expenditure envisaged in the report can be met from the resources available. In recent years there has always been a considerable discrepancy between what is wanted and what is available, leaving the period June to November devoted to bilateral discussions at ministerial level between the Chief Secretary of the Treasury and ministers from the spending departments, and at officer level between the Treasury and its opposite numbers in departments. When these difficulties have been overcome, and they may have to go right up to Cabinet level for decision, the Government issues a White Paper on Public Expenditure normally in January or February. In 1979/80 and 1980/81 the White Papers were delayed until March. It is only then that the DES and the UGC will finally know their main spending budgets, but even at this stage a further round of discussion about peripheral details may be required within the DES before final figures can be given to the UGC. The UGC then undertakes its own allocation exercise and informs universities of their next year's grant in May or June. To make matters more complicated the university financial year is 1 August to 31 July, while the Government's is 1 April to 31 March, so that the period April to August in the following year falls outside the Government's allocation year and therefore outside the Government's projection for inflation. This has the effect of introducing an element of uncertainty as to the level of the grant for the last four months of the university year, particularly in relation to salary awards and inflation factors generally.[1]

The actual process of government resource allocation before final figures are received at the UGC is very long drawn out, extending over nearly three years. The process leading up to the allocation to universities for 1981/82 must have begun in November or December 1979 although the universities did not receive their actual grant figures until July 1981, only a month before their financial year was about to begin. The universities' own resource allocation system must then go into action in order to ensure that their spending units can plan an expenditure pattern for the year. In practice there are two results of such an extended process. The first is that events or changes of policy may occur during the course of the process so as to effect radically the final allocation to universities. In 1979/80, for example, the Secretary of State was talking about 'level funding' for universities (other then the impact of the withdrawal of the overseas student element of the grant) but severe cuts were eventually imposed in 1981/82. We must assume that the chairman of the UGC knew of the change by the summer of 1980 and used it as the unspecified basis of his address to the CVCP in October 1980 quoted above (p.13)[2] The second result is that every participant body in the decision-making chain which has a spending function must anticipate what the final figures may be in order to plan expenditure for the year in question. Within Whitehall what Heclo and Wildavsky describe as the 'village life in civil service society'[3] ensures that spending departments are kept informed of the progress of discussions about departments' estimates. This of course does not help the universities, and, while the UGC and the CVCP exercise a necessary role in passing general messages down the line, until the UGC allocation exercise is completed and actual figures are available, the messages may confuse more than they assist. The need for actual figures is doubly necessary when universities are operating absolutely at the margin and the addition or substraction of £100K may be crucial. The position of the head of a major university spending unit, an experimental science department, for example, is particularly difficult in these circumstances. He needs to plan ahead, particularly in consumables and equipment purchases, and in his policy towards his technical staff as well as his allocation of teaching duties to academic staff, but his budget is right at the bottom of the decision-making process.

He cannot know his allocation until his university has received the grant letter from the UGC, analysed it and decided on an allocation to departments. By that time the new financial year may already have begun and an inefficient pattern of expenditure may necessarily have been embarked upon.

Universities have tended to regard the UGC resource allocation exercise as the significant part of the process, tacitly accepting the allocation to the UGC as a 'given' figure. The CVCP and, no doubt, the UGC have concentrated on bringing pressure to bear on the Secretary of State or the minister who has responsibility for higher education as the key actor in the Government's resource allocation process. An examination of the process shows clearly, however, that at the margins — and in government expenditure terms the margins are very important — the civil servant participants have a significant role. Moreover, as a Treasury Under-Secretary told Heclo and Wildavsky 'you have to recognise that public expenditure is a highly political game', and by that he meant a political game between the spending departments and the Treasury.[4] Higher education as a whole represents only 2.5% of public expenditure and 23% of DES expenditure. Within the public expenditure division of the Treasury higher education is handled by three civil servants, an Assistant Secretary and two Principals, and within the DES, following the merger of the university and advanced further education (AFE) branches, higher education finance is the responsibility of only eight officials, including clerical support, reporting to a Deputy Secretary. At the beginning of the process the UGC must convince the Policy Steering Group in the DES and the Permanent Secretary of DES of the factors which need to be taken into account in reaching an allocation to the UGC. The Policy Steering Group agrees its priorities, after discussion with the Secretary of State, and negotiation with the Treasury is handed over to the DES Finance Branch.[5] In the past, student numbers were a significant feature in the argument but in the current 'expenditure led' situation factors such as purchase and maintenance of equipment, building maintenance and other non-student orientated items are given more weight. The figures are then fed into the PESC cycle, and according to Clive Booth (a former DES official) the UGC, although not formally as closely involved in public expenditure planning as the local authorities, is given the opportunity to comment during the cycle on the various policy options, and its views are put back to ministers and DES officials to consider.[6]

From a timing point of view Booth says it is essential to get policies which require additional spending into the process right at the beginning, that is when the first spending projections are submitted to the Treasury in February in year 2 of the process. The next significant point is the July Cabinet meeting in that year where government spending priorities are agreed. Joel Barnett MP, in his account of his years inside the Treasury says:

'In practice ... the July cabinet, fixing the total expenditure was the crucial one. Both the Treasury and spending ministers recognised it as the key battleground though there might be a lot of skirmishing over the division of "spoils" in bilaterals later on. It is true that in theory, the overall total could be increased at the October meeting, or there could be some "fudging" of the figures but in the main the Prime Minister would be very firm about not allowing a re-opening of this Cabinet decision.'[7]

It is evident that the whole process is highly personalized. Heclo and Wildavsky describe what they call 'family life in the Treasury and village life in Whitehall' and emphasize the strong sense of community, kinship and culture which exist on the civil service network. The negotiations between spending departments and the Treasury are carried out by colleagues with close mutual interests. A departmental finance officer may be expected to find ways of drawing attention to the weaknesses of the case he is arguing as well as the strengths while the Treasury officials may respond by advising that while the case is strong it needs to be put in another way to obtain support. Treasury officials conduct long and critical examinations of new policy proposals, seek to produce less expensive alternatives, are sceptical of arguments based solely on statistics and are wholly opposed to open ended commitments. At the ministerial level too Barnett makes it plain that personalities are equally important: 'More often [expenditure priorities] were decided on the strength of a particular spending minister and the extent of the support he or she could get from the Prime Minister.'[8]

Thus at the governmental level an elaborate resource allocation process takes place conducted on the whole not by people familiar with the effects of policies on the ground, but by civil servants and ministers operating within the established Whitehall conventions. The UGC clearly has a role in this process but only at a fairly remote advisory level, and, with its secretariat drawn from the DES, rather than as in former times from the Treasury, there is no reason to suppose it has an inside track. It is a closed process from which external interests and pressure groups are effectively excluded. Within the process, however, there are important battles to be won and lost. The major battle lost in the past few years was the decision over 'full cost' overseas student fees, widely believed effectively to have been taken in the Treasury within the first week of the new Conservative administration. It is indeed difficult to imagine many battles that have been won on the universities' behalf since 1979. From the universities' point of view there must be a strong presumption that the bargaining process involved in such a system has the effect of curtailing institutional freedom. The participants in the process can have little detailed information of how institutional expenditure works and of the sorts of trade-offs that might or might not be tolerable. Decisions such as the reduction of home and EC student fees in order to prevent a possible over-spend of the non cash limited estimate for government expenditure on student maintenance grants bear the classic hallmark of a centralized decision-making process operating at a considerable distance from the point at which the decision actually takes effect.

The next resource allocation level lies within the UGC. In the past this part of the process has been as inscrutable as that within Whitehall itself but the political pressures arising from the cuts, together with the demands for information by the Select Committee on Education, Science and Arts have resulted in the process leading up to the 1 July 1981 letter being better documented than any previous UGC allocation exercise. In the 1960s and 1970s, in the period of expansion, it is difficult not to believe that within both Whitehall and the UGC student unit costs and a variety of formulae, together with hunch, played a large part in the allocation process. An entertaining series of exchanges in the *Journal of the Royal Statistical Society* in 1976 and 1977 between Dr. W.R. Cook of Laurentian University, Ontario, Sir Frederick Dainton, Professor G.A. Barnard, chairman and member of the UGC respectively, and Drs. Green and Chatfield from the School of Mathematics at Bath, leaves the observer feeling that Dr. Cook was right in his assumption that the UGC used a series of formulae based on projections of student numbers, but wrong in his deductions of the formulae used.[9] Since the formulae were never revealed there was no way that individual universities, which had developed formulae of their own (see Chapter 6), could judge whether their formulae mirrored assumptions made by the UGC. In Ontario the formulae adopted by the provincial government and by the Ontario Council on University Affairs, the Ontario equivalent to the UGC, are public and universities can decide whether they wish to reflect OCUA judgements in their own resource allocation or to substitute their own. Similarly OCUA can judge whether their formulae work at the institutional level and have some yardstick for assessment when universities depart from them. The UGC has always maintained on the contrary the importance of universities not being fettered in their allocation of the block grant by too much knowledge of the mechanism whereby the UGC reached its decisions. There are arguments on both sides but if, as most universities appear to believe in regard to their own resource allocation processes, it is better to disseminate information about their formulae as widely as possible around the institution, it is difficult to see why the same approach does not apply at the UGC allocation level.

Throughout the 1970s an elaborate subject-based committee system existed within the UGC but the speed and complexity of the allocation process made it difficult to build the sub-committees very effectively into decision-making about particular institutions. For the 1981 allocation process, however, the main committee sought to involve the sub-committees very fully. During the first six months of 1980 the UGC held 'dialogue' meetings with universities on the basis of a series of financial scenarios of which the most pessimistic was a 5% cut. In December 1980 the Government announced the abandonment of level funding but the actual recurrent grant figures were not published until March 1981. The main committee considered a number of alternative ways of handling the cuts; reducing the number of institutions, creating a tiered university structure, or an even-handed reduction in resources. In the end it opted for 'a selective approach to the provision of subject places within each subject group.' This brought the subject sub-committees into the centre of the process and led to what the UGC described as an 'iterative process' by which the main committee, or in practice a small group of the main committee, liaised with the sub-committees about the effect which their recommendations would have, when totalled up, on the recurrent grant to each institution. The committee used a battery of statistical indices including GCE 'A' level scores of admitted students, research activity, research studentships, unit costs and the size of university reserves, and it obtained comments from the research councils. The allocations were further affected by decisions to expand student numbers in science, technology and business studies and to maintain medical school intakes at current levels, while bringing a halt to the planned further expansion. Six places in arts and social studies had to be lost to maintain one place in medicine, and between two and three places for one place in science or technology. This led to a requirement for a reduction of overall university student numbers of 5% and a planned cut in staff numbers of about 15% by 1983/84. The effect of these decisions on the universities' own resource allocation processes is described in Chapter 14.[10]

Any description of government or UGC resource allocation systems perhaps inevitably conveys an impression of order and tidiness. It may be that looked at from a top-down point of view, and bearing in mind the scale of the Government's overall resource allocation system, arguments could be adduced to support this. From the universities' point of view, however, the system can seem over extended and frequently chaotic. The question of timing has already been referred to. A system which only delivers a block grant a month before the beginning of the university financial year, especially in a year like 1981/82 when some universities were required to make very substantial cuts in staff and student numbers, is clearly unsatisfactory and encourages inefficient institutional expenditure. It is not easy, however, to see how this can be improved upon unless the date of the Public Expenditure White Paper is moved back to October or November of the preceding year. The universities' requirements in this respect are presumably no different from those of other publicly funded bodies. In practice the situation could be coped with provided there were no sharp changes in government policy and if universities were accorded the full benefit of the PESC planning approach. It must be accepted that quinquennial allocations are now a thing of the past, if only because they are difficult to reconcile with the PESC procedures. But if the UGC, and by extension the universities, could feel confident of being able to plan ahead on the basis of the White Paper projections of government expenditure, some sense of financial security could be re-introduced into the system.

Some of the most serious difficulties, however, have been caused by the inability of the Government's resource allocation process to deal effectively wth the technical problems associated with inflation, particularly in regard to salaries and wages. Under the quinquennial planning system universities had been more or less assured of compensation for inflation on a year by year basis, but in 1973 the UGC announced that it could only guarantee 50% of inflation supplementation for the 1972-77 quinquennium. In 1976 the Government introduced the 'cash limits' approach to public expenditure under which government departments received a 'cash limited' figure calculated at constant prices, which had an inflation element built in but on which departments could not expect supplementary provision during the year. For the universities with salaries accounting for 75% of expenditure this set obvious problems, especially in a period when the general level of university salaries and wages was effectively being controlled from outside either by the workings of an incomes policy or by salary settlements with linked professions in other parts of the public sector of the economy. The university position was further complicated by the fact that, as described above (p.17), the last four months of the university year fell outside the Government's financial year and its inflation estimates. The result was the introduction of two uncertainties: the level of salary rise which Government would permit and therefore fund, and the extent to which the Treasury would fund inflation costs in the 1 April to 1 August period.

This produced a situation where in the first part of the academic year universities were concerned to protect themselves against the Government failing to open its 'cash limits' later in the year. At the beginning of the year, therefore, very strict controls on expenditure had to be urged. Late in the year, however, 'cash limits' were opened and suddenly universities were in receipt of funds which they were usually unable to spend in the period of the year left to them. This imposed a constant schizophrenia in university psychology and did severe damage to the efforts to instil caution into academic departments' expectations of new posts and new developments. Only too often the arrival of substantial funds late in the year made a mockery of previous economy drives and destroyed attempts to inject realism into long-term planning. At the same time Treasury pressure to persuade universities to reduce their reserves, encouraged the commitment of such late allocations to non-recurrent expenditure. In several years this situation was literally chaotic: it encouraged wasteful expenditure, and discouraged realistic future planning. More seriously, it persuaded the university community that severe cuts would not be made in higher education and that vice-chancellors and other senior university figures who had cried 'wolf' every year since 1975 could safely be disregarded.

The White Paper on Public Expenditure published in March 1982 has introduced a refinement of the 'cash limits' approach, in a system called 'cash planning'.[11]   Instead of publishing figures at constant prices, Government has planned public expenditure in cash terms with its assumptions about the rate of inflation built in for each year. Thus 1981/82 figures are up-rated by 4% for pay and 9% for prices for 1982/83, and 1982/83 at an average factor of 6% for 1983/84. In theory this should produce greater stability but much will depend on the Government's ability to control salary costs in the public sector. Failure to do this will produce a situation where further indirect cuts are imposed on universities as a result of salary awards being conceded for which allowance has not been made in the recurrent grant and for which the DES is unable to make further funds available. If indeed a period of relative stability is in prospect, universities should be in a position, using the White Paper projections, to make their own more detailed forward plans based now on financial scenarios rather than on hypotheses based on student numbers.

NOTES AND REFERENCES
1   This description of the operation of the PESC cycle is based on accounts in Heclo, H. and Wildavsky, A. (1981) *The Private Government of Public Money* Second Edition (MacMillan), particularly the Preface, and in Barnet, J. (1982) *Inside the Treasury* (Andre Deutsch)
2   Address by the Chairman of the UGC to the CVCP 24 October 1980.
3   Heclo and Wildavsky op.cit. Chapter 3
4   Heclo and Wildavsky op.cit. p.92
5   This account is based on a chapter by Booth, C. (1982) The roles of the Department of Education and Science and the Treasury, in Morris, A. and Sizer, J. (Eds) (1982) *Resource and Higher Education* (SRHE)
6   Booth op.cit. p.13
7   Barnet op.cit. p.47
8   Barnet op.cit. p.59
9   Cook, W.R. (1976) How the University Grants Committee determines allocations of recurrent grant — a curious correlation *Journal of the Royal Statistical Society* 139 (3) 374. Dainton, F. and Barnard, G.A. (1977) Comments on the paper by W.R. Cook *Journal of the Royal Statistical Society* 140 (2) 199 and 200-209. Cook, W.R. (1977) Curious correlations — a reply *Journal of the Royal Statistical Society* 140 (4) 511-513

THE UNIVERSITY BUDGET

As a preliminary to considering universities' resource allocation processes this chapter is concerned to identify the sources of universities' income and to show how it is actually spent. No account is taken here of UGC grants for expenditure on furniture and equipment, or on major capital works, which are dealt with separately in Chapters 9 and 10 respectively.

Information on both income and expenditure is provided by the universities' annual financial return to the UGC, known as Form 3 (see Annexe, p. 49). It is understandable that a university should use much the same headings as in Form 3 when assessing its income for they describe the sources of that income, but a university is much less likely to adopt the Form 3 expenditure heads for the purpose of planning and controlling its expenditure. Practice varies considerably: there are universities whose annual budget is cast under the Form 3 heads and where control of expenditure follows similar lines, but others have established cost centres suited to their own pattern of activities and mode of management. In such cases the completion of the expenditure sections of Form 3 will require a wholesale reallocation of income and expenditure totals for the year from internal accounts heads to Form 3 heads. Thus the fact that later chapters are devoted to classes of expenditure corresponding to Form 3 categories does not necessarily mean that the universities surveyed actually cast their budgets in the same format, nor that, for example, the 'premises budget' at university A covers exactly the same range of items as that at university B.

RECURRENT INCOME

The total recurrent income of UK universities for the year 1979/80, as returned in Form 3 for subsequent publication in *Statistics of Education* Volume 6, amounted to £1,298 million, which was made up as in Table 1:

A distinction is drawn between General Income and Specific Income because only the former is directly available to spending authorities as part of the budgetary process. Specific Income is, as its name implies, made available for specific designated activities, and is largely reimbursement of costs which would not have been incurred if that service or activity had not been carried out, as for example in the case of grants or contracts from outside bodies for research. It should be noted, however, that where a contract includes an overhead element in addition to identified direct costs, that overhead would be accounted for as a contribution to central

TABLE 1
Total recurrent income to UK universities 1979/80

		Amount £000	Percentage total income %	Percentage general income %
GENERAL INCOME				
i	UGC recurrent grant	822,301	63.3	76.5
ii	Tuition fees and support grants			
	a Home students	170,718	13.2	15.9
	b Overseas and EC students	35,434	2.7	3.3
iii	Endowments, donations and subscriptions	12,060	0.9	1.1
iv	Local authority grants	268	–	–
v	Other income	34,592	2.7	3.2
vi	Sub-total	1,075,373	82.8	100.0
SPECIFIC INCOME				
vii	Computer Board grant	13,018	1.0	
viii	Research grants and contracts	174,257	13.4	
ix	Other services rendered	35,932	2.8	
x	Sub-total	223,207	17.2	
TOTAL INCOME		1,298,580	100.0	

Source UGC Form 3 Return 1979-80

university expenditure and included under General Income (as (v) Other Income). Whether it was actually available for reallocation would, however, depend upon the individual policies and procedures in a given university in regard to overheads (see Chapter 8). Just as the level of activities giving rise to specific income may influence the size of the allocation of UGC recurrent grant to individual universities (see Chapter 4) it may also in turn affect the internal distribution of General Income to spending authorities within each institution.

In describing the universities' income under the heads shown above, it should be noted that one significant source of income does not appear.

Nor does it appear in the *Statistics of Education*, although a return is made under Form 3. That is income from the universities' trading activities, including catering and residences. The UGC requires these activities to be operated on a self-balancing basis with income matching expenditure taking one year with another, and it specifies in some detail what items of expenditure under these headings can be charged against the recurrent grant. Profits on these activities which are not absorbed by losses brought forward from the previous year or carried forward to meet anticipated losses in future years, may be included under General Income as (v) Other Income. To date such an event has been relatively rare, but with the increasing need for universities to look to alternative sources of income to offset the effects of the recurrent cuts in government funding, this situation could change. There is, for example, considerable potential for income generation by the use of residential and catering facilities for the vacation letting trade; universities have for some years looked to this as a means of balancing the account. Henceforth, they may be more concerned to derive an overall profit from it.

It can be seen from Table 1 that, for UK universities as a whole, General Income in 1979-80 represented almost 83% of Total Income. Table 2 tabulates corresponding figures for each of the twelve universities covered in the survey. Here the range is from 77.0% to 92.3% with nine of them contained within the range 83% to 90%. The largest single element of General Income is the UGC recurrent grant which made up 76.5% of total General Income for all UK universities in 1979-80. It will be seen from Table 3 that the corresponding figure for the twelve universities covered in the survey is spread fairly evenly over the range 71.2% to 79.0%.

The other major element of General Income is tuition fees. Fees have become increasingly significant to the universities, the percentage they contributed to total income rising from 5% in 1973/4 to 16% in 1979/80. Given their importance in the total budget, the manipulation to which the fee element has been subject since 1979 has added considerably to the difficulties experienced by universities in their budgeting process. The effect of the introduction of 'full cost' fees for overseas students beginning courses on or after 1 September 1980 has already been referred to in Chapter 2. A further change is the virtual halving of the home undergraduate fee to £480 in the academic year 1982-83 together with a compensating increase in the UGC recurrent grant (matched by a reduction in the Rate Support Grant to LEAs). This change has been introduced by the Government to protect its cash limits policy, which might otherwise be undermined if universities were tempted by fees in excess of marginal cost to mitigate their financial plight by the admission of home students above the UGC's target numbers, which would thus generate additional public expenditure on student maintenance awards.

Of the remaining elements, the most significant is Other Income which includes the contributions to central expenditure (overheads) referred to above, rents received for the letting of rooms, and interest earned by the investment of temporary cash balances on the General Funds account. During a period of high interest rates the investment of temporary cash balances represents a significant element of the income under this heading.

The income items (iii) and (v) in the table above have always been important to universities, both because they offer a significant indication of a university's reputation in the outside world, and because, not being subject to the same restraints on usage as the block grant, they provide some small measure of flexibility and independence. Item (iv), Local Authority, was an important item prior to the 1970s when local authorities made regular and often substantial contributions to university income. In recent years, however, the contributions have substantially diminished both in real terms and as a proportion of university income. Historically the UGC block grant has always been regarded, in spite of its size, as a deficiency grant. It was the residual component in a package of total resources which in the UGC view was the appropriate figure in a given year for each individual university, having regard to such factors as the previous level of support, student numbers, the relative unit cost of students in different disciplines, the quantity and quality of research activity, the capacity of its buildings, and any scope for economies of scale. Subject to the constraints of the total grant made available by the Government, the UGC made allocations to universities which reflected these and other criteria, and which took into account a university's potential General Income from sources (ii) to (v). For as long as the grant continued to be regarded as a deficiency grant, there was little or no incentive to seek to augment subsidiary sources of income since the benefit remained with the individual institution, as distinct from the system, only until such time as it took the UGC to update its expectations and make a corresponding reduction in future grant allocations.

Over the last decade, however, the attitude of the UGC to additional income has modified. A letter to vice-chancellors in 1970 gave a first indication of change. In giving guidance on the question of its treatment of income from donations and endowments the chairman stated that consequential reductions in grant were not automatic, that each case was treated on its merits, and that a reduction in grant was only likely if income from these sources was applied to produce a level of costs in particular areas which seemed to the Committee to be unreasonably high, even after all the circumstances had been taken into account. But it was not until a letter from the chairman to vice-chancellors in May 1982[1] that the concept of deficiency funding could be said to have been abandoned, and the universities could feel confident that the effort put into raising additional funds would accrue directly to the institution concerned and not the system as a whole. In the letter the chairman outlined the Committee's approach to reduced funding in the period 1981-1984 and stated specifically:

TABLE 2
Total recurrent income to twelve universities 1979/80

	A			B			C			D			E			F			G		
	£000	%	%	£000	%	%	£000	%	%	£000	%	%	£000	%	%	£000	%	%	£000	%	%
GENERAL INCOME																					
i UGC recurrent grant	7,694	61.3	71.7	8,949	66.7	75.0	28,578	60.8	79.0	5,985	64.1	71.3	8,427	63.2	71.2	27,026	65.3	76.6	19,531	62.3	74.7
ii Tuition fees and support grants																					
a Home students	2,155	17.2	20.1	2,315	17.3	19.4	5,495	11.7	15.2	1,410	15.1	16.8	2,569	19.3	21.6	5,808	14.0	16.5	4,236	13.5	16.2
b Overseas and EC students	362	2.9	3.4	430	3.2	3.6	835	1.8	2.3	690	7.4	8.2	446	3.3	3.8	1,269	3.1	3.6	870	2.8	3.3
iii Endowments, donations and subscriptions	3	–	–	–	–	–	463	1.0	1.3	–	–	–	77	0.6	0.7	120	0.3	0.3	323	1.0	1.3
iv Local authority grants	1	–	–	18	0.1	0.2	–	–	–	–	–	–	–	–	–	36	0.1	0.1	1	–	–
v Other income	513	4.1	4.8	217	1.6	1.8	821	1.7	2.2	312	3.3	3.7	319	2.4	2.7	1,023	2.5	2.9	1,187	3.8	4.5
vi Sub-total	10,728	85.5	100.0	11,930	88.9	100.0	36,192	77.0	100.0	8,397	89.9	100.0	11,838	88.8	100.0	35,282	85.3	100.0	26,148	83.4	100.0
SPECIFIC INCOME																					
i Computer Board grant	59	0.5		117	0.9		903	1.9		38	0.4		87	0.7		276	0.7		357	1.1	
ii Research grants and contracts	1,566	12.5		1,328	9.9		6,688	14.3		909	9.7		988	7.4		4,644	11.2		4,404	14.1	
iii Other services rendered	192	1.5		46	0.3		3,205	6.8		–	–		422	3.1		1,174	2.8		446	1.4	
iv Sub-total	1,817	14.5		1,491	11.1		10,796	23.0		947	10.1		1,497	11.2		6,094	14.7		5,207	16.6	
TOTAL INCOME	12,545	100.0		13,421	100.0		46,988	100.0		9,344	100.0		13,335	100.0		41,376	100.0		31,355	100.0	

	H £000	H %	H %	J £000	J %	J %	K £000	K %	K %	L £000	L %	L %	M £000	M %	M %	UK £000	UK %	UK %
GENERAL INCOME																		
i UGC recurrent grant	12,401	72.4	78.5	20,498	67.1	77.3	15,375	63.2	74.5	9,875	58.9	73.6	10,715	63.6	73.8	822,301	63.3	76.5
ii Tuition fees and support grants																		
a Home students	2,379	13.9	15.0	4,249	13.9	16.0	3,753	15.4	18.2	2,430	14.5	18.1	2,934	17.4	20.2	170,718	13.2	15.9
b Overseas and EC students	694	4.1	4.4	952	3.1	3.6	929	3.8	4.5	617	3.7	4.6	340	2.0	2.3	35,434	2.7	3.3
iii Endowments, donations and subscriptions	–	–	–	332	1.1	1.3	24	0.1	0.1	4	–	–	70	0.4	0.5	12,060	0.9	1.1
iv Local authority grants	–	–	–	7	–	–	–	–	–	–	–	–	–	–	–	268	–	–
v Other income	329	1.9	2.1	481	1.6	1.8	564	2.3	2.7	497	3.0	3.7	462	2.8	3.2	34,592	2.7	3.2
vi Sub-total	15,803	92.3	100.0	26,519	86.8	100.0	20,645	84.8	100.0	13,423	80.1	100.0	14,521	86.2	100.0	1,075,373	82.8	100.0
SPECIFIC INCOME																		
i Computer Board grant	159	0.9		220	0.7		253	1.1		56	0.3		146	0.9		13,018	1.0	
ii Research grants and contracts	1,106	6.5		3,575	11.7		3,307	13.6		3,206	19.1		1,968	11.7		174,257	13.4	
iii Other services rendered	52	0.3		238	0.8		109	0.5		79	0.5		210	1.2		35,932	2.8	
iv Sub-total	1,317	7.7		4,033	13.2		3,669	15.2		3,341	19.9		2,324	13.8		223,207	17.2	
TOTAL INCOME	17,120	100.0		30,552	100.0		24,314	100.0		16,764	100.0		16,845	100.0		1,298,580	100.0	

Source Statistics of Education Vol. 6 1979-80

'Many universities are seeking ways of attracting additional income from external sources. The Committee would wish to encourage this. Income so raised will not lead to a consequential reduction in grant.'

Thus the removal of the disincentive to raising additional income under General Income categories (iii) — (v) combined with the universities' new freedom to maximize their income by the recruitment of overseas students at 'full cost' may lead, at least in the more entrepreneurially minded universities, to an interesting readjustment of the relationship between the different elements making up the overall category General Income. The most optimistic might take the view that success in such efforts may make universities somewhat less vulnerable to the vagaries of successive governments' economic policies.

EXPENDITURE

Table 3 shows a breakdown of the expenditure of all UK universities in 1979/80 under the heads adopted by the UGC for publication of Form 3 data and Table 4 shows the corresponding figures for the twelve universities covered in the survey.

It should be emphasized that just as the figures shown in Tables 1 and 2 exclude some sources of income, so the figures in Tables 3 and 4 do not represent the universities' gross expenditure. First, many small items of income are netted off against expenditure (the most substantial instances are DES/SED grants for adult education, and NHS capitation fees for health services); secondly, capital expenditure met from UGC non-recurrent grants and from private funds is omitted; thirdly, trading accounts (catering, residences, farms, arts centres) feature only in so far as subsidies are paid to them from general funds.

Table 4 permits a comparison both between the universities surveyed and the national average of percentage expenditure under each of the Form 3 heads. Chapter 6 discusses the extent to which universities make use of comparative data of this sort in their resource allocation processes, but it should be emphasized here that a simplistic analysis of expenditure such as that in Table 4 would have severe limitations as a normative tool; it should be regarded only as indicative of the different patterns of expenditure that exist. Two points illustrate the need for caution in interpretation. Firstly, the expenditure from specific income is mainly incurred in academic departments and is far from the total cost of the activities in question. Under the dual support system the costs of the 'well-found laboratory', including the principal investigator's salary, along with most of the overheads of administration and accommodation are financed from general income. Secondly, the subject mix of departments and students has a strong bearing on the pattern of expenditure. The UK average departmental expenditure per FTE student in veterinary science is nearly four times as much as per FTE student in an arts subject. Most of

TABLE 3
Total recurrent expenditure in UK universities 1979/80

		Amount £000	Percentage total income %	Percentage general income %
EXPENDITURE FROM GENERAL INCOME AND COMPUTER BOARD GRANT				
a	Academic departments	594,944	46.1	54.8
b	Libraries	53,788	4.2	5.0
c	Other academic services	47,009	3.6	4.3
d	General educational expenditure	29,267	2.3	2.7
e	Administration	79,176	6.1	7.3
f	Maintenance of premises	215,641	16.7	19.9
g	Student amenities & welfare	21,157	1.6	1.9
h	Miscellaneous	22,435	1.7	2.1
i	Capital expenditure from income	21,985	1.7	2.0
	Sub-total	1,085,402	84.2	100.0
EXPENDITURE FROM SPECIFIC INCOME (excl. CB grant)		204,064	15.8	
TOTAL EXPENDITURE		1,289,465	100.0	

Source UGC Form 3 Return 1978-80

the 'extra' cost of 'expensive' subjects appears as academic departmental expenditure from general income. Hence the fact that a university with many students in expensive subjects spends a lower percentage than a predominantly arts based university on student amenities and welfare, for example, does not necessarily mean that the quality of the provision is any the less.

A more sophisticated computer-based analysis of expenditure using the Form 3 data has been developed by Taylor (see Chapter 6). Under this method a calculation can be made for each university of what its expenditure would have been under each of the Form 3 heads had it spent at the GB average level (excluding London, Oxford, Cambridge and the Business Schools). The GB average level for each university is arrived at by an elaborate process of correction which takes into account student load, the

TABLE 4
Total expenditure in twelve universities 1979/80

	A			B			C			D			E			F			G		
	£000	%	%	£000	%	%	£000	%	%	£000	%	%	£000	%	%	£000	%	%	£000	%	%
EXPENDITURE FROM GENERAL INCOME AND COMPUTER BOARD GRANT																					
a Academic departments	6,167	50.0	57.9	6,055	46.1	51.4	19,721	42.1	52.0	3,990	43.0	47.7	7,211	53.5	58.5	20,596	50.7	59.0	14,995	48.2	56.8
b Libraries	557	4.5	5.2	626	4.8	5.3	1,553	3.3	4.1	472	5.1	5.6	783	5.8	6.4	1,161	2.9	3.3	1,278	4.1	4.8
c Other academic services	488	4.0	4.6	591	4.5	5.0	2,783	5.9	7.3	430	4.6	5.1	423	3.1	3.4	1,057	2.6	3.0	1,251	4.0	4.7
d General educational expenditure	316	2.6	3.0	293	2.2	2.5	896	1.9	2.4	110	1.2	1.3	227	1.7	1.8	697	1.7	2.0	638	2.0	2.4
e Administration	765	6.2	7.2	963	7.3	8.2	2,411	5.1	6.4	790	8.5	9.4	745	5.5	6.0	2,403	5.9	6.9	1,760	5.7	6.7
f Maintenance of premises	1,714	13.9	16.1	2,444	18.6	20.7	8,826	18.9	23.3	1,681	18.1	20.1	2,224	16.5	18.0	6,727	16.6	19.3	5,310	17.1	20.1
g Student amenities & welfare	239	1.9	2.2	357	2.7	3.0	589	1.3	1.5	246	2.7	2.9	519	3.8	4.2	599	1.5	1.7	443	1.4	1.7
h Miscellaneous	44	0.4	0.4	181	1.4	1.5	476	1.0	1.3	326	3.5	4.0	95	0.7	0.8	880	2.2	2.5	476	1.5	1.8
i Capital expenditure from income	363	2.9	3.4	278	2.1	2.4	686	1.5	1.8	316	3.4	3.9	102	0.8	0.9	770	1.9	2.2	265	0.8	1.0
Sub-total	10,654	86.4	100.0	11,788	89.8	100.0	37,941	81.0	100.0	8,361	90.2	100.0	12,329	91.4	100.0	34,890	86.0	100.0	26,416	84.6	100.0
EXPENDITURE FROM SPECIFIC INCOME (excl. CB grant)	1,674	13.6	—	1,342	10.2	—	8,888	18.9	—	909	9.8	—	1,156	8.6	—	5,700	14.0	—	4,677	15.4	—
TOTAL EXPENDITURE	12,328	100.0	—	13,130	100.0	—	46,830	100.0	—	9,271	100.0	—	13,484	100.0	—	40,591	100.0	—	31,093	100.0	—

EXPENDITURE FROM GENERAL INCOME AND COMPUTER BOARD GRANT

	H £000	H %	H %	J £000	J %	J %	K £000	K %	K %	L £000	L %	L %	M £000	M %	M %	UK £000	UK %	UK %
a Academic departments	8,562	50.6	54.3	15,579	51.7	59.2	12,058	51.4	60.1	7,314	45.1	56.6	7,411	44.1	50.6	594,944	46.1	54.8
b Libraries	563	3.3	3.6	1,189	3.9	4.5	748	3.2	3.7	824	5.1	6.4	787	4.7	5.4	53,788	4.2	5.0
c Other academic services	564	3.3	3.6	832	2.8	3.2	1,003	4.3	5.0	518	3.2	4.0	502	3.0	3.4	47,009	3.6	4.3
d General educational expenditure	286	1.7	1.8	683	2.3	2.6	313	1.3	1.6	299	1.8	2.3	294	1.7	2.0	29,267	2.3	2.7
e Administration	1,304	7.7	8.3	1,809	6.0	6.9	1,229	5.2	6.1	1,221	7.5	9.4	1,168	6.9	8.0	79,176	6.1	7.3
f Maintenance of premises	3,006	17.8	19.1	5,033	16.7	19.1	3,611	15.4	18.0	2,196	13.5	17.0	2,907	17.3	19.8	215,641	16.7	19.9
g Student amenities & welfare	348	2.1	2.2	550	1.8	2.1	238	1.0	1.2	312	1.9	2.4	352	2.1	2.4	21,157	1.6	1.9
h Miscellaneous	443	2.6	2.8	361	1.2	1.4	280	1.2	1.4	170	1.0	1.3	157	0.9	1.1	22,435	1.7	2.1
i Capital expenditure from income	698	4.1	4.4	280	0.9	1.1	594	2.5	3.0	77	0.5	0.6	1,081	6.4	7.3	21,985	1.7	2.0
Sub-total	15,774	93.3	100.0	26,316	87.4	100.0	20,074	85.6	100.0	12,931	79.7	100.0	14,659	87.2	100.0	1,085,402	84.2	100.0
EXPENDITURE FROM SPECIFIC INCOME (excl. CB grant)	1,132	6.7	–	3,799	12.6	–	3,383	14.4	–	3,285	20.3	–	2,162	12.8	–	204,064	15.8	–
TOTAL EXPENDITURE	16,907	100.0	–	30,114	100.0	–	23,457	100.0	–	16,217	100.0	–	16,820	100.0	–	1,289,465	100.0	–

Source Statistics of Education Vol. 6 1979-80

distribution of that load between subject areas and the level of study. Actual expenditure by the university can then be compared with the GB average level, and expressed as a percentage of it, as set out in Table 5. (The expenditure heads are divided somewhat differently from the Form 3 out-turn for reasons of internal analysis in the university concerned.)

TABLE 5
Percentage relationships in university A between actual and GB average expenditures

Expenditure head	Actual £000	GB average £000	Actual as % of GB
Academic salaries	4,341	4,738	91.6
Departmental support staff	1,089	1,444	75.4
Departmental consumables and equipment	737	613	120.2
Library	556	594	93.8
Central university computer	252	292	86.3
AVA	209	164	127.4
General educational expenditure	317	331	95.8
Administration and central services	765	856	89.4
Ord. repairs and maintenance	533	688	77.5
Heat, light, power, telephones	467	657	71.1
Cleaning and custody	380	524	72.5
Miscellaneous premises	334	641	52.1
Facilities and amenities	239	285	83.9
Miscellaneous	72	248	29.0
Capital from income	363	294	123.5
Totals	10,654	12,369	86.0

The information presented in Table 5 becomes more readily assimilable when presented graphically in the form of a chart. These charts have become known as 'Taylor squares'. In Figure 1 a square representing the GB average expenditure for university A is constructed giving widths proportional to percentage expenditure in the different areas. Figure 2 takes the percentage of the GB average level of expenditure represented by university A's actual expenditure and reconstructs the square by extending or truncating columns accordingly. Figure 3 tidies up the square by arranging the percentage columns in rank order, and also shows by an arrow the overall expenditure relationship of the university with the GB average, which in the case of

FIGURE 1
Projected recurrent expenditure at university A if at GB average level

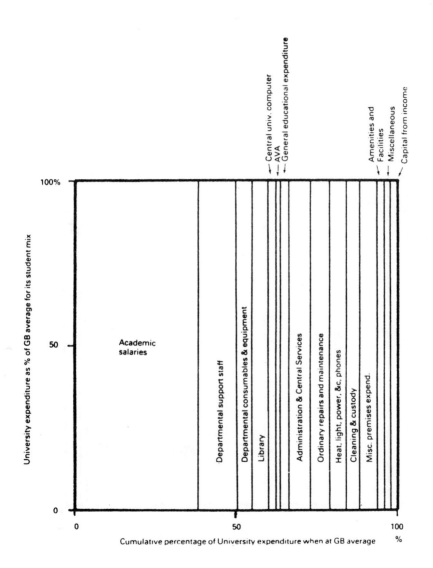

Source Derived from UGC Form 3 out-turn

FIGURE 2
Actual recurrent expenditure at university A as percentage of projected
expenditure at GB average level

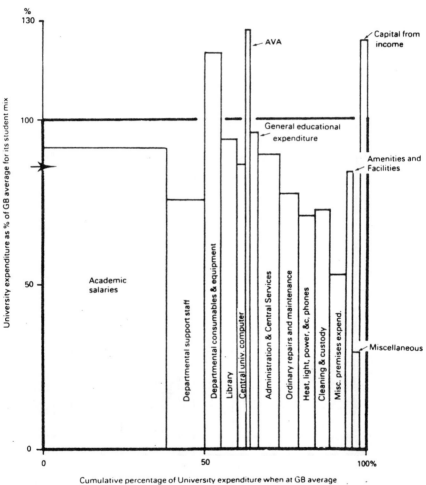

Source Derived from UGC Form 3 out-turn

FIGURE 3
Taylor square for university A

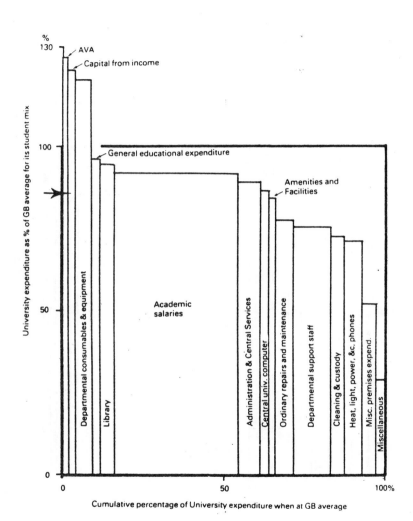

Source Derived from UGC Form 3 out-turn

FIGURE 4
Taylor square for university B

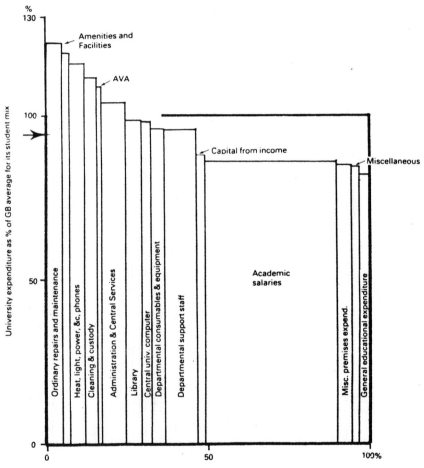

FIGURE 5
Taylor square for university C

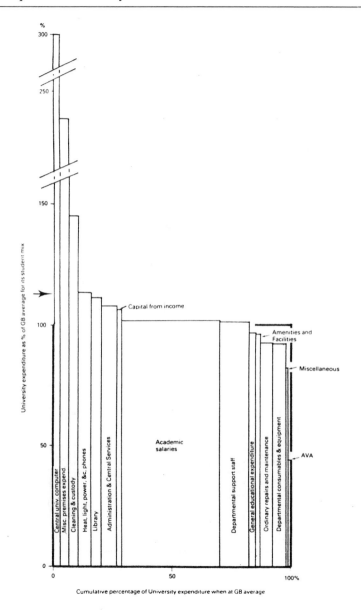

Source Derived from UGC Form 3 out-turn

FIGURE 6
Taylor square for university D

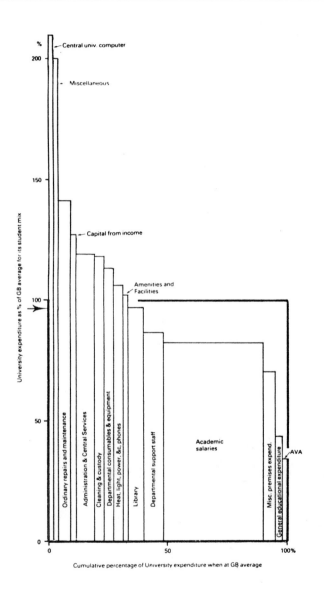

Source Derived from UGC Form 3 out-turn

FIGURE 7
Taylor square for university E

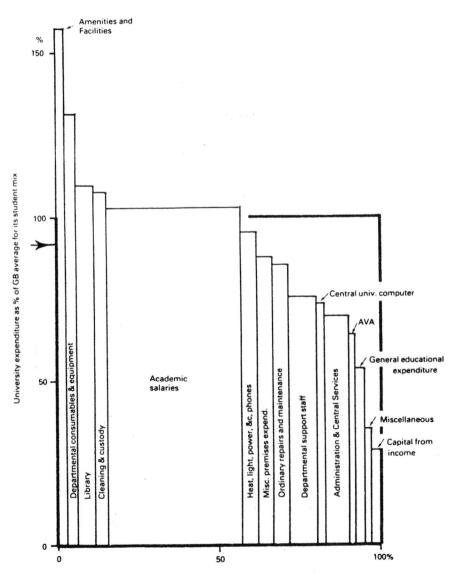

Source Derived from UGC Form 3 out-turn

FIGURE 8
Taylor square for university F

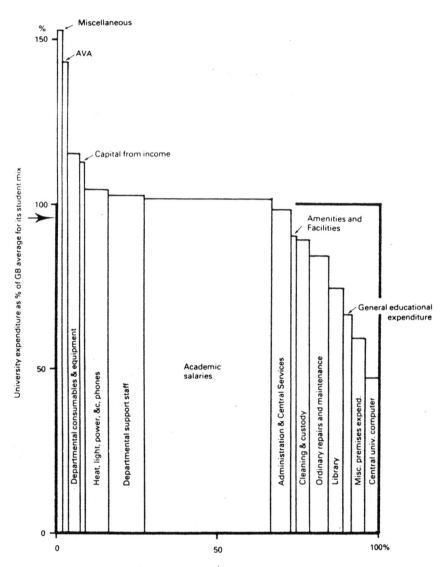

Source Derived from UGC Form 3 out-turn

FIGURE 9
Taylor square for university G

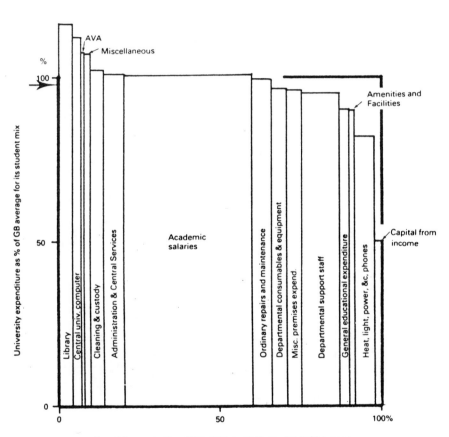

Source Derived from UGC Form 3 out-turn

FIGURE 10
Taylor square for university H

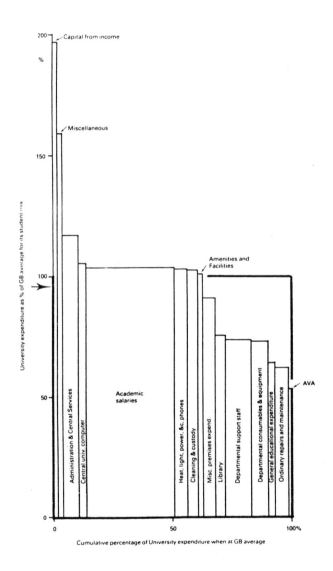

Source Derived from UGC Form 3 out-turn

FIGURE 11
Taylor square for university J

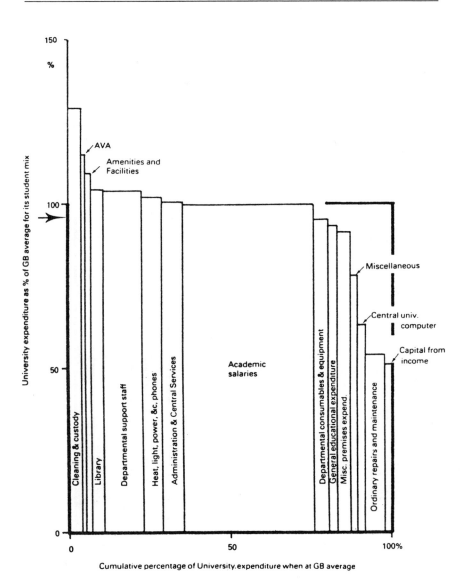

Source Derived from UGC Form 3 out-turn

FIGURE 12
Taylor square for university K

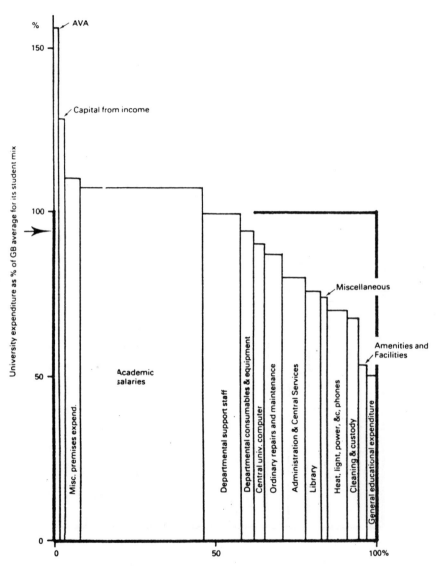

Source Derived from UGC Form 3 out-turn

FIGURE 13
Taylor square for university L

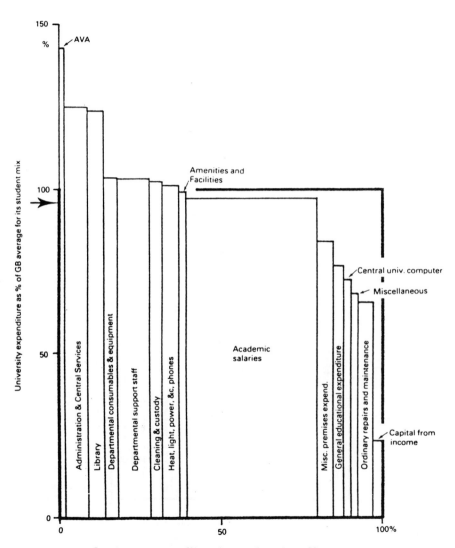

Source Derived from UGC Form 3 out-turn

FIGURE 14
Taylor square for university M

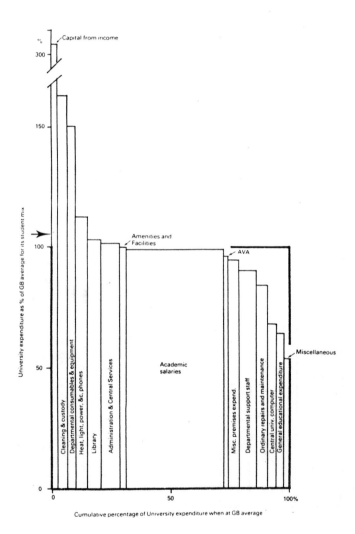

Source Derived from UGC Form 3 out-turn

university A is 86%. Thus at a glance it is possible to see areas of 'overspend' and 'underspend' in terms of the national average, and to identify, by looking at those columns which are higher than the arrow, and those which are lower, areas which are receiving preferential treatment within the institution, and those being underprivileged. For instance, even though Academic Salaries in Figure 3 are below the GB average, they are above the arrow, and hence relatively privileged within the university in comparison to Support Staff salaries which fall below the arrow. Figures 4 to 14 give comparable charts for a sample of other universities. All costs relate to the 1979-80 financial year.

The Taylor square provides a useful analysis of expenditure within individual institutions and permits a considerable variety of inter-university comparisons. We do not suggest, however, that the technique should drive the allocation of resources in any particular direction. Its value is that it serves to prompt questions about why an institution deviates from the norm, and to demonstrate patterns of expenditure which may not have been fully appreciated. Its main purpose is to provide an institution with the facility to re-examine its expenditure priorities in the light of its overall pattern of expenditure and the pattern of expenditure elsewhere.

ANNEXE: UGC FORM 3

Reference is made on a number of occasions to UGC Form 3. Form 3 is the annual accounting document which all universities are required to return to the UGC (in addition to their printed accounts). Form 3 is the only source for reasonably comparative information as between universities on their financial affairs. It has a remarkably long ancestry because the main parts of Form 3 in 1981/2 are the result of gradual adaptation of the financial report form introduced by the UGC for its first year of operation, 1919/20. Evident in that form are today's broad distinctions between recurrent and capital expenditure, and between general income and expenditure, specific income and expenditure, and subsidiary accounts for trading activities; evident also are many of the specific heads and their contents. Completion of Form 3, which must be audited by the universities' external auditors, is a condition of receiving Exchequer grant, and its categories must be graven on the hearts of generations of university accountants.

The layout of the form is currently in the process of being amended, and the following description relates to the revised layout.

Form 3 consists of a number of tables:

1 Student statistics
2 Recurrent income
3 Expenditure of recurrent income
4 Expenditure of income from research grants and contracts and for services rendered

5   Catering and residences accounts
6   Earmarked grants
7   Allocated and unallocated revenue balances
8   Equipment and furniture grants

Many of the tables show the information by eighteen subject groups which at present are as follows but which are also currently under review:

1   Education
2   Medicine
3   Dentistry
4   Allied to Medicine
5   Engineering/Technology
6   Agriculture
7   Veterinary Science
8   Biological Sciences
9   Mathematics
10 Computer Science
11 Physical Science
12 Other/Combined Sciences
13 Business Management
14 Social Studies
15 Architecture and Planning
16 Other Professional and Vocational Studies
17 Languages
18 Other Arts

Table 1: Student statistics shows details of undergraduate, taught post-graduate and research postgraduate numbers and full-time equivalent loads by the eighteen subject groups.

Table 2: Recurrent income shows under general income the following items (many being sub-divided):

The UGC grants
Academic fees and support grants
Endowments, donations and subscriptions
Grants from local authorities and the Computer Board
Income from extra mural classes

Under specific income appear the following major items:

Research grants
Research contracts
Income for services rendered

Table 3: Expenditure of recurrent income analyses the expenditure by five groups of staff and expenses of:

Academic departments by the 18 subject groups
Academic services by libraries, central computers, central educational technology units and the like
General education expenditure
Premises
Administration and central services
Staff and student amenities and facilities
Capital expenditure met from recurrent income
Pensions
Transfer to equipment and furniture grant
Miscellaneous

Many of the items are again sub-divided.

Table 4: Further analyses research grants and contracts expenditure by the eighteen subject groups.

Table 5: Summarizes the catering and residences accounts.

Table 6: Shows details of earmarked grants.

Table 7: Sets out allocated and unallocated revenue balances.

Table 8: Shows equipment and furniture grants.

The universities' returns are made available to all universities. In addition, a summary which has recently been redesigned is published by the UGC and the Universities' Statistical Record (USR).

NOTES AND REFERENCES
1   UGC circular letter 10/82, 20 May 1982 (para 7(a))
2   Taylor, B.J.R. (1982) Resource allocation in UK universities *The AIR Professional File* 11, 1-8

THE INTERNAL DECISION-MAKING PROCESS

The changing external financial climate has put universities' internal decision-making procedures for resource allocation under considerable pressure. An examination of their constitutional structures and procedures shows that a large number of universities are now questioning whether the methods evolved and adopted for resource allocation in the 1960s and early 1970s can deal adequately with the very different circumstances of the 1980s.

THE SITUATION IN 1979/80

Table 6 gives a summary of the structure of the main resource allocation committee concerned with the overall university budget in each of the universities surveyed in 1979/80. Table 7 gives similar information about the main committee concerned with the allocation of resources within the academic sector at each of these universities in 1979/80. In the tables we have attempted to identify those committees which are in practice the prime movers, rather than those which carry formal responsibility. Any such analysis must, of course, involve a considerable simplification and leave out of account a number of bodies which fulfil a significant resource allocation function.

Anything more than the most cursory examination reveals the variety and complexity of the arrangements by which institutions with broadly the same objectives and functions have attempted to deal with the problem of resource allocation. In general, ultimate responsibility for the management of finance lies with the Council (in Scotland, the Court) while responsibility for academic matters, in other words the university's principal objectives of teaching and research, lies with the Senate. Resources must therefore ultimately derive from the former body but are clearly vital to the latter; the way in which the two bodies relate to each other in this context is therefore crucial. How is the potential gulf to be bridged, and how is a balance to be struck in resource allocation between directly academic purposes (salaries of academic staff, departmental grants, etc.) and non-academic expenditure (such as administration and maintenance and security of buildings)?

Broadly speaking, two main devices have been employed. In some universities a single body is concerned with the allocation of resources in some detail, that is to actual spending units, in both the academic and the non-academic sectors: constitutionally, this body may be a committee of the Council or, recognizing the interest of the Senate, it may be a joint committee of both governing bodies. In others, the Council fulfils its responsibility through a committee which makes a 'block grant' to the academic side and allows the Senate, or a committee of Senate, discretion (which may or may not amount to virtual freedom of action) in allocating resources to faculties, schools or departments, to other academic units, and to other academic purposes such as research funds and vacation grants.

At five of the universities we surveyed, the arrangements approximated to the first pattern (ie a single body dealing in some detail with allocations for academic and non-academic purposes). In two of these the key committees were joint committees of the Senate and the Council: one of these committees reported to both the Senate and the Council, its allocations requiring Council approval; the other reported to the development committee of Senate and the finance board of Council, its allocations requiring the approval of both, as well as the Senate and Council themselves. In two other universities the key committees were sub-committees of the finance committee and some or all categories of their allocation decisions were subject to the approval of the local equivalents of finance committee and Council.

Six universities fell broadly into the second pattern where a Council committee makes a 'block grant' to the academic sector. At five of these the key committee for the overall university budget was the finance committee, which reported to the Council and in four cases required Council approval for some or all categories of allocations. At the sixth university, the key committee was a sub-committee of the finance committee, whose allocations required the approval of both the finance committee and the Council. At only one of the six universities did the detailed allocations made by Senate level committees within the academic section of the budget require (in theory at least) the approval of the finance committee or of the Council.

Evidence from the survey suggests that, at most of the universities, it was usual for the resource allocation proposals of the key committees listed in Table 6 to 'pass through' the finance committee (where this was not itself the key committee) and the Council without serious challenge or modification. The 'long-stop' powers of the Council, as the body with ultimate responsibility for the management of university finances, were therefore seldom used to change significantly the decisions of lower committees.

The relationship between resource allocation and other decision-making structures is also important because it helps to define the criteria on which resource allocation is based. Resource allocation implies the existence of institutional objectives, whether embodied in an academic plan, or in decisions of Senate and Council, or enshrined in some intangible way in Charters and Statutes. The most significant structural link is obviously with the academic planning process. In some universities planning (which may mean determining student targets or explicit priorities amongst departments for development or contraction) and resource allocation may be carried out by one committee. In others the two functions are kept separate. Where they are separate the question must arise as to the extent to which resource allocation is decided simply on the basis of the expressed need of the spending units balanced against the resources available or by reference to priorities agreed elsewhere. We found a considerable variety of systems and sub-systems in operation. Often where planning and resource allocation were separate operations the committee memberships were overlapping to provide co-ordination. The Vice-Chancellor might be chairman of both bodies and the committee officers might also be common. On the other hand there were instances of a lack of co-ordination where resource allocation seemed to be quite seriously uncoupled from the planning process. In one university the resource allocation body appears almost to stand apart from the formal constitutional structure of the university, taking its own decisions without apparently much reference to other bodies.

RECENT DEVELOPMENTS

About half the universities surveyed either had already made significant changes in their resource allocation procedures during the latter half of the 1970s or have made such changes or begun major reviews of their procedures since 1980. Annexe A (p. 67) gives four examples of developments and reviews which have taken place since 1979: they are illustrative only and do not purport to be comprehensive. A particular feature during the later 1970s was the establishment at many universities of new committees and procedures for reviewing vacant posts and determining which should be frozen or filled. Annexe B (p. 74) gives examples of committees for reviewing vacancies which were in existence in 1979/80.

It would perhaps be gratifying, from the universities' point of view, to be able to say that all the important changes which have taken place in recent years were the result of deliberate planning or intelligent anticipation. Some of them had, however, the character of a pragmatic response to immediate needs, though they were not necessarily less effective for that reason.

In many cases the incentive for change clearly came from the need for financial retrenchment. More specifically, the introduction of procedures such as those illustrated in Annexe B were a response to a situation in which it was necessary to leave unfilled a substantial number of posts becoming vacant, still the most commonly practised means of reducing expenditure. In a few instances a newly appointed Vice-Chancellor or Principal has evidently been the driving force behind structural change, perhaps because as a newcomer with recent experience of different systems he is more ready and able to take a critical view of an established structure.

Four main strands are discernible in the changes which have taken place or been discussed during the past five years or so:

A   The belief, or the experience, that as the financial climate worsened, fairly large groups consisting mainly of academic staff with vested interests would find it increasingly difficult to make critical judgements on such matters as vacancies.

B   The feeling that an over-rigid division of the university budget into 'academic' and 'non-academic' sectors could lead to lack of balance, and that all expenditure should come under a similar degree of scrutiny, preferably by a single body.

C   The need for a closer co-ordination of academic decision-making and academic resource allocation.

D   The view that devolution of resource allocation to bodies closer to the 'coal face' would lead to more effective use and management of scarce resources.

It will be noted that some of these factors — eg B and D — can (though need not necessarily) pull in different directions. It must be emphasized that there is no uniform pattern among universities, that seemingly similar trends may stem from very different roots, and that even within a single institution there may be developments working in what appear to be contrary directions. Universities may sometimes be over impressed by mechanisms and procedures employed at other universities. This 'grass is greener' syndrome, which may result from more general dissatisfaction about the level of resources available, can lead to confusion and disillusion. There is a danger that some other institutions' resource allocation procedures can look attractive either because they produce a priority ordering which the external observer would wish to see realized in his own university or because they fit some preconceived set of ideas about decision-making and who takes part in it.

The extent to which financial pressures have led to, or are leading towards, greater centralization and concentration of decision-making and less participation on the part of academic staff generally, is a matter on which there is conflicting evidence. There can be little doubt that, faced with the need to cut back on developments and in some cases make absolute reductions in expenditure, sometimes on a very short time scale, many universities found it necessary to develop emergency measures to deal with what was seen as an emergency situation. In one university, for example, in which resource allocation rests with an unusually large and mainly representative committee, two very small sub-committees were set up in the mid-1970s to deal with academic and academic-related vacancies so that any spending authority wishing to fill a vacant post had to obtain permission from one of the sub-committees. Within the university it seemed to be generally agreed in principle that such a procedure could only be temporary and that a fundamental review of the allocation mechanism was essential, but the parent committee apparently proved incapable of proceeding with the review. A further group comprising only four members (two of them laymen) carried out a review of the whole of the university's income and expenditure in 1980/81.

A large university which has traditionally operated on the principle of making a block grant to Senate and allowed considerable freedom to the academic side in utilizing resources has recently established a new Council committee with the expressed purpose of achieving greater control over the balance between 'academic' and 'non-academic' expenditure. Yet in the same institution considerable energy is being devoted to the dissemination of information on resource allocation and forward planning, and to the continued discussion of these matters at Faculty level; indeed the head of the university is on record as saying that he is determined to preserve normal constitutional procedures to the maximum extent possible.

The picture becomes even less homogeneous if we consider the situation in a third university. Here resource allocation was for many years based on a single committee of about a dozen members which effectively allocated resources to all the institution's fifty or so spending authorities. Now consideration is being given to the devolution of responsibility for resource allocation to Faculties, not only with the object of greater co-ordination of academic decision-making and resource allocation but also because devolution is thought likely to enable Faculties to bring their own requirements and priorities more directly to bear upon resource allocation problems. It remains to be seen whether this change, which illustrates the recognition of the need for a closer articulation between academic and financial planning, but which also seems to run counter to the movement towards concentration and centralization evident in some other universities, will indeed come about.

This chapter is concerned mainly with the decision-making processes for the academic sector of universities' budgets: around 67% of expenditure from General Income in UK universities (see Table 3, p. 31). It is worth remarking, however, that on the non-academic (Council) side, in such areas as administration and the central services for example, although there are clear constitutional arrangements for the final approval of overall allocations, there has not been the same development of elaborate mechanisms and committee processes for the detailed assessment of budgetary claims as on the academic side. As Chapter 11 shows more fully, detailed decision-making on the non-academic (Council) side often actually takes place outside the formal committee structure. Assumptions and judgements made by the various officers concerned in drawing up the budget have often already been built in by the time the budget is exposed to the body within the decision-making structure which has the authority to approve it. To this extent senior officers, often working through the Vice-Chancellor, may exercise considerable influence in the determination of budgets in the non-academic area. It remains to be seen how far the attempts to co-ordinate and assess priorities between the academic and non-academic budgets will lead to any serious erosion of the relatively powerful position of some administrative officers in these areas.

CONSTITUTIONAL ISSUES

Although British universities have similar, even common, objectives, and employ to some extent comparable, though not identical, means to achieve these objectives, local variations and circumstances can easily be quoted to nullify sweeping generalizations, or to bemuse the researcher with so many footnotes that the main text is forgotten. A commentary on the constitutional structures involved in resource allocation is inevitably a speculative and provocative business, rather than a synthesis. In 1970 John Fielden was arguing that the increasingly sophisticated management techniques involved in the so-called managerial revolution in university administration could have an impact on constitutional arrangements:

'Many of the tasks will seem to imply an increasing centralization of university decision-making. This must be avoided at all costs and the preeminence of devolution and participation must be assured. The increasing sophistication of the central administration will be an improved service to the academic decision maker, not a shackle.'[1]

That comment could be extended to a situation where the need to take difficult and sensitive decisions may encourage the concentration of authority in the hands of a small number of people. It almost seems to have been assumed in the late 1970s when questions of filling or freezing vacancies in a tight financial situation were discussed that such decisions were best left to the Vice-Chancellor and some small group of senior academics and administrators; the decisions were going to be difficult, and rather than have an unseemly squabble among academic colleagues it was better to let the agony and if necessary the odium rest with the men at the top.

More positively, it could be argued that the reaction seen in many institutions in the late 1970s and not so much defeatist as recognizing that the nature of the decisions to be taken required the creation of as impartial a group of individuals as possible. These should be able, and were required by virtue of some office which they held in the institution, to stand back from their departmental or personal interests, so that the decisions taken would be generally seen to be reasonable, equitable and necessary. This perception of the decisions was all the more likely if the group operated on the basis of generally agreed criteria and generally agreed methods of calculation and provided for the reasonable advocacy of a special case which any particular sector wished to pursue. The consensus might also rest on some general understandings about a policy which had been made explicit to each member of the community and which therefore formed an almost unconscious background for the evaluation of the decisions of any so-called controlling group.

There are a number of reasons for thinking that this approach has becomes less acceptable, at least since universities received their July 1981 letters from the UGC. The decisions now and in the future may be not merely 'to fill or not to fill' but 'to fire or not to fire'. Such decisions may in turn be linked to decisions about the survival of particular disciplines within the university. Extraordinarily sensitive decisions may also have to be taken about the deliberate reduction of staffing and other resources in some subjects in order to create room for the importation of 'new blood' needed to maintain the vitality of others or to permit some new lines of development within the same or different areas. Recent evidence seems to show that members of university staffs, and members of Senates, may be very much less inclined to leave decisions of that kind to the Vice-Chancellor, or even to a special committee which the Senate itself may have helped to set up. Those universities which, with the best of intentions, produced by extraordinary procedures master plans within three or four months of the July letters may turn out to have given themselves a much rougher ride than those which went through the painful process of argument through the normal constitutional procedures; clearly the position varies to some extent in relation to the severity of the cuts imposed on individual universities, but not all those bearing the worst percentage reductions in support have experienced more difficult constitutional and procedural problems than universities much less badly hit.

Almost equally relevant may be the greater public awareness of universities' problems and the greater degree of availability of information within universities. Increasingly, UGC pronouncements about university funding, student numbers and academic plans are regarded as public material, and so, more slowly, are universities' individual responses. Increasingly too, the UGC is encroaching on crucial aspects of academic policy: not only can it now enforce particular home student number targets on universities in the arts and science areas but it is also ready to exert strong pressure on universities to phase out or reduce activities in specific subject areas: a situation which, when coupled with the reduction of resources to universities and the extent of their past economies, greatly limits the traditional freedoms of universities. British universities are becoming, willingly or not, more sensitive to the political environment, a situation which is already such a feature of the US scene. Within the period of one quinquennium universities have moved from expansion and relative affluence to contraction and extreme stringency; if the frustration within universities has been restrained largely because those most directly concerned were well informed about the causes of their frustration, the implication must be that universities should make every effort to ensure the widest possible dissemination of information in the future. A more fundamental consideration is that if universities exist to develop and project knowledge and freedom of thought and expression, should their own procedures and mechanisms of self-government fail to reflect this in such a crucial area as resource allocation? If this is true for institutions, is it not also true at the national level? There is an evident contrast between the openness of data bearing on resource allocation within universities and the closed procedures used by the UGC when reaching its decisions in 1981.

It is tacitly assumed by most universities that the process of resource allocation requires discussion and judgement in committee, rather than merely knowledge and the routine application of formulae. The number of people actively involved in resource allocation, however, at least at the stage where major decisions are being taken, is invariably small. Moodie and Eustace have suggested that:

'there is a greater need for bargaining and compromise, indeed for "horse-trading", in the painful process of pruning bids and hammering out a university budget than in other areas of academic decision-making. Such "in-fighting" is most easily conducted, and with least harm to social cohesion, by relatively small numbers of people each of whom must be armed with some authority, not only to speak for a group's interests but to negotiate and (if need be) to accept defeat.'[2]

We found that the combined strength of the two or three main resource allocation committees is most unlikely to exceed 40 or 50 in any university, and in many cases is considerably less; this is out of a total community, even in a small university, of several thousand staff and students. Restricting our analysis to academic staff and specifically to resource allocation for academic purposes, we found that in the universities surveyed the number of staff involved in the key committees rarely exceeds 20.

It is usually argued that smaller committees are more efficient and are better at taking difficult decisions than larger bodies. They are, of course, criticized from outside the decision-making group for being unrepresentative or for being so small that full discussion with a wide range of views expressed does not occur. Against this it must be said that large and seemingly democratic committees can sometimes, particularly under strong chairmanship, behave almost like rubber stamping bodies in which complex and sensitive issues and possible alternative courses of action are seldom discussed seriously. This situation may arise partly because of the inhibition that many individuals feel about participating in discussions as committee size increases: in consequence their willingness to 'go along with' or their reluctance personally to oppose proposals submitted to them may be greater on large committees than on small ones. It may also arise because there is a greater likelihood that the available time will be frittered away on unimportant matters or on educating members who have not read or understood their papers. Nevertheless, even if a large committee normally behaves like a rubber stamp, the knowledge that the awkward question may be asked and the rubber stamp withheld can still have a powerful influence on the formulation of policy.

The question of the wider dissemination of information has already been touched on and a good deal of information about resource allocation for academic purposes is frequently made available to university Senates, though rarely, except perhaps in a crisis, discussed there in other than general terms.

The composition and size of the Senates in the universities varies greatly. With one or two exceptions, however, roughly one in five to one in seven members of *teaching* staff is a member of Senate: a somewhat lower proportion results if research staff are taken into account. One of the exceptions raises interesting questions: when the present constitution of this Senate was determined in the early 1960s, the model which it was hoped to avoid was that of the large assembly comprising the professoriate ex officio and hardly anybody else: instead the Senate was to be small, and therefore effective, and to have a majority of its members elected, a revolutionary concept at the time. The arrangement resulted, however, in an unusually small proportion of staff being involved in policy-making and its operation tends in practice to reinforce the power of the Vice-Chancellor, Pro-Vice-Chancellors and Deans over the elected members, who serve for only three years at a time, hardly long enough to learn what is afoot before their membership comes to an end. By a constitutional quirk, moreover, the problem is exacerbated by the uneven incidence of rotation among elected members which occurs not in tidy proportions of one-third each year but one-third in the first year, two-thirds in the second, and none in the third.

THE VICE-CHANCELLOR

The role of the Vice-Chancellor in resource allocation is an interesting study in itself and illustrates the extent to which the representation of the formal machinery may fail to give an accurate indication of how things are done in practice.

At one end of the spectrum we found one university in 1979/80 where the Vice-Chancellor did not appear even as an ex officio member of his university's academic resource allocating body, a situation since changed as a result of a modification of the committee structure. At the other extreme, another Vice-Chancellor appeared to exercise a virtual monopoly of the supply and distribution of management information prepared for him by one administrative officer answerable to him alone, and to use this monopoly in the major resource allocation body, whose status is in any case advisory to the Vice-Chancellor and not answerable to Senate or Council. At nine of twelve universities the Vice-Chancellor was chairman of the major academic resource allocating body and at a further two he was a member of that body.

Four of the universities entrenched the Vice-Chancellor as chairman of the major resource allocating committee responsible for the overall university budget; four other universities provided in the chairmanship of the lay treasurer an arrangement which might be thought more accurately to reflect the theoretical constitutional relationship between the 'lay' and the 'academic' element in university government.

Typically, therefore, the Vice-Chancellor is a member of the chief resource allocating bodies, as well as of most other important committees, and normally he is buttressed by one or more Pro-Vice-Chancellors. Whatever his formal involvement in committees, however, there can be little doubt that, if he wishes, the Vice-Chancellor is in a uniquely powerful position to influence resource allocation. In him are brought together the academic prestige and experience which give leadership among his academic colleagues and the administrative and management expertise derived from the support he draws from the Registrar and his staff — sometimes underlined by the presence of administrative staff responsible to the Vice-Chancellor alone. Even in a very large university, where the most active Vice-Chancellor cannot achieve detailed knowledge of all that is going on, or even all he needs to know to meet the demands placed upon him, the Vice-Chancellor almost inevitably knows more than anyone else in the place, and has ready access to any information needed to fill gaps in his knowledge.

The Vice-Chancellor's dominant position in resource allocation is probably enhanced by two further factors. The first is that he is the prime recipient, and the prime interpreter within his university, of the increasingly crucial and delphic 'guidance', both formal and informal, which issues from the UGC. The second is that he gains vital background information from his membership of the CVCP which has become increasingly involved in the resource allocation sphere at national level, as a source of analyses, as a forum for inter-university discussion and as a spokesman and negotiator for the universities. The combined effect of these factors on the Vice-Chancellor's role is unlikely to be outweighed by the greater public availability of information about UGC policy and intentions through the medium of the press.

ADMINISTRATIVE STAFF
The traditional view of the role of administrative staff in British universities has been to see them as a kind of academic civil service[3] advising university committees, servicing the mechanism of university government, and implementing decisions for which others take constitutional responsibility. There is no doubt, however, that in resource allocation as in other aspects of university management the Registrar or Secretary and his staff may, like the civil servant in government, play a crucial role. They provide the continuity; and the position of the Registrar may be less open to threat than that of the Vice-Chancellor, since the latter is more likely to be in the limelight and the political firing-line. Administrative staff have, or at least have access to, the background against which decisions are to be made; above all, in the context of resource allocation, they are probably in possession of more information than any other group or individual involved, with the exception of the Vice-Chancellor himself. In some areas of the university budget, as will be seen elsewhere in this study, the Registrar himself may exercise a large measure of control; in relation to the budget generally, the Registrar, the Finance Officer and their staffs provide the information and advice on the basis of which decisions will be taken, and are

likely to have ready access to the ear of the Vice-Chancellor or whoever may be in the chair at vital meetings. The extent of that influence, and the manner of its exercise, vary widely, however, and the personality of the individuals concerned is obviously of considerable importance. A fairly recent development in some universities has been where the growing importance or seniority of officers with particular professional expertise has made the Registrar more the chairman of a group of senior officers than someone holding personal responsibility for particular administrative actions.

A refinement which would merit further study is whether there is any significant difference in the presentation of advice, and the outcome, between those universities in which the Registrar has primacy over the Finance Officer/Bursar and those in which the two posts are of equal status: at least nominally, the former situation would appear to put the Registrar individually into a more influential position. However, even where the Registrar has primacy, the Finance Officer has direct access to the Vice-Chancellor and may be directly consulted by him. It may well be that in a period of financial retrenchment in contrast to the period of expansion, the role of the Finance Officer and his staff in the area of resource allocation becomes much more important vis-à-vis that of staff in the academic planning office.

THE PLACE OF THE LAYMAN

All of the twelve universities surveyed had a traditional bi-cameral structure of government with a lay dominated Council (or in Scotland, Court) and an academic Senate. In seven of the twelve universities the chairman of the main resource allocation committee concerned with the overall university budget was a layman, usually the university Treasurer. Laymen constituted between one-quarter and one-half of the membership of that committee at all but four universities, where the proportion was lower.

During our investigations only a few universities commented in any detail on the extent of the influence exercised by laymen on the main resource allocation committee. The proportion of laymen on a committee is unlikely to provide a reliable measure of their influence on policy-making. On the one hand, there is likely to be a higher incidence of non-attendance and of irregular attendance among lay members than among academic members. Moreover, laymen are normally very careful not to get drawn into academic questions which are seen as falling within the sphere of the Senate, whereas their academic colleagues have less reason for inhibition. On the other hand, laymen often have the advantage of a wider experience of business matters and a better appreciation of national and regional attitudes than do academics. When these advantages are allied to a long standing association with the close knowledge of the workings of the university a layman's views may carry considerable weight, not least where other parties are divided in their views. Experience also suggests that laymen may tend to see more clearly than academics the need for expenditure on such items as maintenance and student services as well as having a valuable contribution to make to income-generating and capital-raising ventures. We found at least one instance where there had been lobbying of influential laymen by academics disgruntled over the allocation of resources to their academic area. Local tradition and expectations appear to have a good deal to do with the extent of active participation and influence by laymen.

It seems reasonable to expect that their influence should become greater as resources become scarcer. The change from expansion to level funding or contraction enhances the importance of Council's role as the body with ultimate responsibility for the university's financial viability. Decision-making about the balance between and within the academic and non-academic sections of the budget is made more difficult and critical. And, given the Council's responsibilities as employer, a time of contraction may also see a blurring (however unwished for by all concerned) of the division between 'Senate' and 'Council' matters: for example, the Senate may decide to phase out a particular academic activity but, if this involves compulsory staff redundancies, the final decision to declare individuals redundant is within the province of the Council, not the Senate. The Councils of at least two universities in 1981/82 have actually referred back recommendations for compulsory redundancy.

A further role for the layman may be the injection of senior managerial experience. This is a more controversial aspect. In one technological university not part of our detailed study where severe cuts had to be made the *Financial Times* reports the Vice-Chancellor and the Secretary General of the university as paying tribute to the important role of the chairman of Council, who was also chief executive of a major public company, in managing the cuts situation. The latter is quoted as saying that 'the critical factor was not him but his managerial experience'. He went on:

'The reason why so many universities can't organise themselves to cope with reduced income is not that their staff are stupid,' he adds. 'It's because they haven't had any practice at it. Until lately they just sent in their bills and they got paid. But I've had experience in such things, and it has taught me that top management must respond by deciding quickly what's to be done, spelling it out and sticking to it, staking their own jobs on the result if necessary. You've got to be decisive and determined.'[4]

We do not believe this reflects a typical view of universities amongst laymen, but in at least one other university local authority members of the university Council complained that their own experience of retrenchment was being made too little use of in a period of financial stringency. The fact remains that, however it is used, lay experience in handling resource allocation in a period of contraction is itself an important resource for universities to draw upon.

DEANS AND HEADS OF SCHOOLS

The significance of Deans of Faculties, Heads of Schools, and similarly titled academic staff varies considerably in resource allocation procedures. In some institutions they are virtually ignored in resource allocation; allocations are made direct to a lower tier, normally the department, and the Dean is simply not involved. In other cases the Dean may act as spokesman for his academic area in presenting a bid to the resource allocating body but may again be by-passed when the allocation is made. Elsewhere, however, the situation may be very different, and in a large university practising a devolved system the Dean may find himself in at least as powerful a position in relation to departments in his Faculty or School as is the Vice-Chancellor himself in relation to the faculties. At the same time he may play a significant part in the allocation of resources in the university as a whole. In one university consideration was being given in 1981/82 to deans being granted the power to 'hire and fire' almost on a US pattern.

STUDENTS

At five of twelve universities the main resource allocation committees concerned with the overall university budget included one or more student representatives. Only two of the key committees concerned with the academic section of the budget included student representatives. We found no evidence that students played a significant role in resource allocation except as advocates for expenditure on areas of their own interest. This is perhaps surprising when one recalls the large claims advanced in the 1960s and early 1970s for student participation in university government, but the rapid turnover of student members of committees, usually on a year to year basis, militates against student members developing a sufficient understanding of the technical and procedural aspects of the processes to make an effective contribution.

THE STRUCTURAL LINK BETWEEN ACADEMIC DEVELOPMENT AND RESOURCE ALLOCATION

In the majority of the universities surveyed the constitutional arrangements appeared to provide at least the opportunity for the consideration of desirable academic developments or necessary academic retrenchment and resource allocation to come together in the same committee. In at least one of the minority of universities which had separate committees dealing with academic planning and resource allocation, moves are actively under way to bring about a unification. It may be relevant that in another similarly organized university where no such move is evident the all-important resource allocating body is equally responsible to both Council and Senate. There can be little doubt that whereas in the 1960s academic planning could proceed with little more than a courtesy reference to resources, confident in the belief that resources would be available for whatever new developments might be proposed, the climate of the late 1970s and early 1980s has stimulated the much more pragmatic conclusion that academic planning is now dominated by the resource situation. The creation of a structural link between academic policy-making and resource allocation will also serve to counteract what seems in some institutions to be a hiatus caused by the fact that whereas resource allocation is necessarily a 'top-down' process, desirable academic plans are more likely to spring from initiatives at departmental or faculty level and tend to follow a 'bottom-up' procedure.

CENTRALIZATION AND DEVOLUTION IN RESOURCE ALLOCATION

It is important to distinguish between the decision-making structures for planning and resource allocation, and the extent of financial responsibility and control which the allocating bodies at the various levels actually exercise. The example usually given of a devolved system is where the faculty or school of studies is interposed as a separate decision-making level between the central university bodies and the departments or primary spending units. In such systems the faculty is not only responsible for academic decision-making but also has a financial function, bidding for resources, receiving a budget and reallocating it to spending units. By contrast, highly centralized systems are normally identified as being those where central bodies deal directly with departments in matters of finance, with little involvement by the faculty.

If, however, we think about devolution specifically in terms of how a budget is handled, which body is responsible for controlling it, and to what extent the budget holder has the freedom to manipulate the various heads of expenditure within the budget and the right to carry forward year-end balances, then the picture can be very different. For example, viewed in this light, Cranfield (see Chapter 13) is par excellence an institution with a devolved budgetary system, although the faculty has little financial role to play. At this institution allocations of resources are made directly to the departments but once a department receives its budget it has a very considerable degree of autonomy in that it may organize expenditure from that budget as it thinks fit on staff, consumables, minor works, etc. Provided that the department runs its programme and meets its objectives without running into deficit the control of all types of expenditure is left to the head of the department concerned. Along with this freedom to control heads of expenditure goes a parallel requirement that departments pay their own way, all centrally provided services from accommodation to cleaning being rechargeable to the departments which, in order to survive, must sell their own skills and services in the market place. Less extreme examples can be found of universities which tightly control resource allocation centrally at the level of finance committee but nevertheless operate a high degree of budgetary devolution by allowing considerable freedom of virement at the department level. Similarly, where, as is commonly the case, the central allocation committee is small, the relatively low academic staff participation at that level may be to some extent offset by a high degree of participation at the lower, devolved, level.

Advocates of financial devolution use arguments of the following kinds:

1   The quality of decision-taking is better nearer the 'coal face', where the criteria used are likely to reflect more sensitively local needs and priorities.
2   The rewards of 'good housekeeping' are tangible and benefit those responsible for achieving it (where there is carry forward of balances as well as a considerable freedom of virement).
3   Faculties are best able to make judgements about quality and decisions about new developments, and devolution therefore provides a better environment for the encouragement of excellence and innovation.
4   The extent of staff participation is increased and the sense of equity enhanced.

Those who argue against financial devolution tend to do so on grounds such as:

1   The administrative cost of the system could offset the gains from better 'housekeeping'.
2   Devolution engenders a rigid compartmentalism which intensifies the disposition to take a departmental or faculty rather than a university view.
3   Where devolution is to a faculty level, decision-making on resource allocation at the university level may become more difficult, especially at a time of declining resources, because faculties are reluctant to take greater than pro rata cuts: with the result that any advantages arising from dirigiste decisions about priorities *within* given budgetary areas (if indeed such dirigisme takes place) are likely to be offset by the increased difficulty of transferring resources from one area to another or indeed of finding resources for completely new development.
4   A powerful central body is in a position to judge the academic priorities of the institution as a whole and to avoid much sterile argument among closely related vested interests.

It is sometimes argued that, in theory, a highly centralized system is more likely to produce mediocrity than devolved decision-taking because a central body is insufficiently close to the primary units to be able to assess, and therefore give special support to, quality and promise. The argument tends to be reinforced where the centralized system relies on an extensive use of norms and formulae so that qualitative judgements are replaced by decisions arrived at mechanistically.

Against this, however, supporters of a centralized system point out that there are advantages in decision-taking being carried out at a slight distance from the proponents of particular cases and that there is a tendency to shirk critical decisions when they have to be taken by people working in close proximity with one another. In the abstract the argument is not capable of resolution. Much clearly depends on the traditions which universities set themselves for firm decision-making.

It is probably true that a centralized system in good hands can do more positive good for an institution than a devolved system where inevitably there will be variations in effectiveness between the different spending units. On the other hand, the pervasive influence of a few outstanding individuals working close to the subjects concerned can clearly transform a particular academic area more effectively than can a centralized system.

We also wondered whether size had any relevance in this context but found no correlation between size of institution and kind of decision-making process. Of the two largest universities, one was centralized, one decentralized; the two smallest were both highly centralized. It is interesting to note however that, faced with the difficulty of planning and allocating for retrenchment, several universities were considering changing their style. One of the hardest hit is considering how to decentralize while one of the larger civics is seeking to centralize decision-making more than it has previously done.

ANNEXE A: SOME RECENT DEVELOPMENTS IN PROCEDURE

Detailed examples follow of some significant structural developments or reviews which have taken place since 1979. These are illustrative only and do not purport to be comprehensive. Universities are identified by the same letters as in Tables 6 and 7.

In 1980 university D began a review of its arrangements for resource allocation, which were widely felt to be unsuitable for dealing with the problems of financial contraction. Characteristics of the existing arrangements included strong Council control over the budget, a complex and insufficiently co-ordinated structure of committees each concerned with the allocation of different sections of the budget, and insufficient attention by its academic development committee to the cost implications of proposals for academic development. One solution widely canvassed and on the point of approval was the transfer to Senate of the administration of a substantial element of the budget. A further important thread in the discussion was the belief that departments needed to be given more autonomy in resource allocation decisions and allowed greater powers of virement, rather than having most decisions taken for them by central committees. The effect of the July 1981 letter, however, was to put all these ideas back into cold storage and to involve the academic development committee more in financial policy.

Late in 1979 at university F the planning committee established a

TABLE 6
Comparison of the major resource allocation committees (overall university budget

University	Title of committee	(Lay) Treasurer	Vice-Chancellor	Pro-Vice-Chancellor(s)	Other academic	Lay	Students	Others	Total
A	Finance executive sub-committee		1A	1		2x .		2E*	6
B	Investment and financial review committee	1A	1	2		2x		4E*	10
C	Finance committee		1			1x		10EA*	12*
D	Resources sub-committee of the finance committee	1A	1	1	1x + 2E	1E			7
E	Resources allocation sub-committee		1	2A	6x + 3E				12
F	Planning committee	1	1	3	13x + 6E (s)	2x + 4E (c)	1x + 2E (u)	1x	34
G	Finance and general purposes committee	1A	1	2	3E	4E	2x		13
H	Finance and general purposes committee	1A	1	1		1C	2x	6E*	12
I	Resources committee*	1	1A	2	2E (s)	1x		2E**	9
J	Finance committee		1		5E	2EA	1x		9
K	Budget sub-committee of the finance committee	1	1A	3					5
L	Finance committee		1	1	4E	3x + 2EA	3E	X	15

* ** See notes A = chairman x = ex officio E = elected or appointed (By
X = Registrar/Secretary Y = Finance Officer Z = other members of
indicate categories of persons, not precise titles which vary from university to

n twelve universities 1979/80

Source of appointed members (if not Council)	Years of service of appointed members	Serviced by	Other non-members normally attending	Notes
Finance committee	No specific period	Z	X, Y, 1Z	* 2 members of finance committee; academic or lay
	1R	Y	X, 1Z	* 4 members appointed by Council; academic or lay
	2R	2Z	X	* No rules about proportions of academic and lay. In 1979/80 5 of 10 were academic, 5 lay. Chairman and vice-chairman are always lay ** Plus up to 2 co-opted (normally inc president of Students' Union
	1R	Y	X, 3Z	
Academic planning committee		Z	X, Y, 5Z	* Sub-committee of the finance committee
Council, Students' Union, Senate	1R (c), 1R (u), 2R (s)	Z	X, Y, 5Z	* Joint executive committee of Senate and Council
	1R	Y	V, X	
	3R	X	Y, 2Z	* Usually 3 of 6 academic, 3 lay
Senate	3R	Z	X, Y	* Joint committee of the finance board and the development committee of Senate ** In 1979/80 both were appointed by Council, and were lay
	3R*	Y	X	* Lay convenor appointed for 4 years
		X	Y	
Senate: 4 academic members; Student rep; Council: 3 student members	4R (academic and lay) 1 (student member)	Y		

Council unless otherwise stated) C = co-opted R = renewable W = Librarian
administrative staff (s) = Senate (c) = Council (u) = Students' Union *Headings*
university

TABLE 7
Composition of the major resource allocation committee (academic section of the

University Title of committee Membership of committee

		Vice-Chancellor^X	Pro-Vice-Chancellor^X	Deans^X	Other academic	Lay	Students	Other	Tot
A	Planning committee of Senate	1A	1	5*	11E	2x	1x + 3E		24
B	Senate development committee	1A	2	1	9E*				13
C	Development and estimates committee	1	3A	3	6E				13*
D	Committee of Deans	1A	1	9	2x				13
E	Resources allocation sub-committee of the finance committee	1	2A	2E	6x + 1E				12
F	Planning committee*	1A	3	10	3x + 6E (s)	3x +4E (c)	1x +2E (u)	1x	34
G	Estimates and grants committee		1A	4*	4E				9
H	Vice-Chancellor's advisory committee	1A	2	3*					6
I	Resources committee*	1A	2		2E	2x		2E**	9
J	Educational policy committee	1A	2	9	12E				24
K	Budget sub-committee of the finance committee	1A	3			1x			5
L	Development committee of Senate	1A	2		4E				7

* ** See notes   A = chairman   x = ex officio   E = elected or appointed (By
X = Registrar/Secretary   Y = Finance Officer   Z = other members of
indicate categories of persons, not precise titles which vary from university to

udget) in twelve universities 1979/80

source of appointed members (if not Senate	Years of service of appointed members	Serviced by	Other non-members normally attending	Notes
5 elected by Senate. 6 elected by Faculties or Faculty groups. 3 students selected by students from various Faculty areas	5R	X		* Including 4 chairmen of Boards of Faculties. See Note 1, p. 72
	3	X	Y, 1Z	* In 1979/80 there were 10, not 9, in this category, inc. 9 Deans
	3R	Z	X	* And up to one co-opted member
		Z	V, X, Y, 1Z	See Note 2, p. 72
2 Deans and one other academic nominated by academic planning committee		Z	X, Y	See Note 3, p. 72
Council, Students' Union, Senate	1R (c), 1R (u), 2R (s)	Z	X, Y, 5Z	* Joint executive committee of the Senate and Council
	1R	V	Y, Z	* Chairmen of Faculty Boards
		X	2Z	* Area chairmen. See Note 4, p. 72
Council**	3R	Z	X, Y	* Joint committee of the finance board and the development committee of the Senate ** In 1979/80 both these members (appointed by Council) were lay
	3R	V	X, Y, 2Z	See Note 5, p. 72
		X	Y	See Note 6, p. 72
	4R	V	X, Y	See Note 7, p.73

Council unless otherwise stated)   C = co-opted   R = renewable   W = Librarian
administrative staff   (s) = Senate   (c) = Council   (u) = Students' Union   *Headings*
university

NOTES TO TABLE 7

1   The planning committee is not solely concerned with the academic area. It also controls most categories of staff establishment (maintenance, portering and self-financing areas being the main exceptions) and has separate vacancy groups for clerical, technical and academic staff with a membership of four, six and nine respectively.

2   Responsibility for resource allocation in the academic sector is divided between several committees. The Committee of Deans is responsible for recommending the allocations of money for new (including unfrozen) academic and non-academic posts. In this connection it itself receives recommendations from a variety of committees each concerned with particular categories of staff, including (for example) the academic development committee, which makes recommendations about chair vacancies and is also the body responsible for making recommendations to Senate about student intakes and the academic plan of the university. The Committee of Deans is *not* concerned with departmental running costs and equipment: departments submit bids for these direct to the departmental grants sub-committee of the finance committee.

3   In the academic area, the resources allocation sub-committee is (since June 1980) responsible for making annual allocations for running costs to individual departments. The staff policy committee is responsible for splitting between academic and non-teaching posts, and for apportioning to individual departments any sum provided in the approved overall budget for spending on additional staff: in this connection, the committee receives recommendations from a staff committee (academic) and a staff committee (non-teaching).

4   The Vice-Chancellor's advisory committee is not solely concerned with the academic area. It can, if it wishes, comment on all sections of the university budget.

5   The educational policy committee is advised by a planning group consisting of eight members of the committee, none of whom may be a dean.

6   In the academic area, the budget sub-committee of the finance committee recommends in detail allocations of departmental grants to, and additional spending on non-academic staff in individual departments and also a total academic staff establishment for the year in question. The allocation of new academic posts to departments is determined by recommendations from the senate planning committee to the senate. The senate planning committee is a committee of 13 members including the Vice-Chancellor (chairman),

three Pro-Vice-Chancellors, five Deans of Schools, the Dean of Students, one other academic member and two students.

7   In practice, the development committee is not solely concerned with the academic area. It normally has the opportunity to comment upon a draft outline budget covering both the non-academic and the academic sectors and from time to time takes the initiative in proposing programmes of economy cuts extending beyond the academic area.

---

working group comprising the Vice-Chancellor, a Pro-Vice-Chancellor and the Chairman and Vice-Chairman of the Council to consider the effects upon the size, activities and standards of the university of the anticipated gap by 1983/84 between income and existing expenditure commitments. Its first report, in June 1980, was more concerned with academic structures in general terms than with finance. In the Autumn term 1980 it was enlarged by the addition of the heads of the two principal academic units and asked main spending units how they would absorb a hypothetical 20% cut in their budgets. The group was responsible for producing the detailed discussion document in response to the UGC's letters of 1 July 1981, commented on the replies from spending units, and supervised the preparation of the university plan for 1983/84 that had been approved by the Senate and the Council in early 1982 and on which the return to the UGC on staffing levels in 1983/84 was based.

At the beginning of the 1979/80 academic year the Senate of university G established a working party on academic strategy, chaired by the Vice-Chancellor and with a membership partly ex officio and partly ad personam. The committee was intended to provide an overall strategy within which the committees responsible for planning and resource allocation could operate and it established a 'university data base', a range of detail which the university could use in assessing the quality of individual departments or courses in order to assist decisions on resource allocation. The working party experiment was criticized on two grounds: first that it did not have sufficient links with the existing planning and academic resource allocation bodies and second that the ad personam members were insufficiently representative of Senate or other interests. The working party had been established for only one year in the first instance and was replaced by a new joint planning and resource allocation committee under the chairmanship of the Vice-Chancellor, which had on it all the members of the planning and resource allocation committees with the single addition of the President of the Students' Union.

The joint committee considered the July letter and recommended Faculty targets to the Senate for subsequent comment by the Faculties. These comments were reviewed by the planning committee which itself recommended the detailed targets to Senate. The resource allocation committee was given a target of savings by the finance committee and was required, as was the Senate, to obtain finance committee's permission for any posts to be advertised.

University J has replaced the former finance committee with a resources committee, which has the task of reviewing the resources available to the university and allocating them on a block grant basis. The resources committee has a membership of 10, including two lay members, and is chaired by the Vice-Chancellor. It has two sub-committees: a finance sub-committee and a committee on non-academic expenditure, the first chaired by a layman and the second by the Vice-Chancellor. The re-organization follows a change of Vice-Chancellor and is intended (inter alia) to improve control over non-academic expenditure and improve the university's ability to respond flexibly to the new financial situation. Under the former finance committee it was customary for officers to prepare the budget on the basis of a fixed 70:30 split between academic and non-academic expenditure. The new resources committee is no longer committed to the 70:30 convention.

ANNEXE B: COMMITTEES FOR REVIEW OF VACANT POSTS
Examples follow of committees and groups which in 1979/80 were responsible for reviewing vacant posts and for deciding or recommending whether these should be frozen or filled. Universities are identified by the same letters as in Tables 6 and 7 and Annexe A (p. 67).

A   The Planning Committee, which controls the majority of staff (maintenance, portering and self-financing areas being the main exceptions), has separate vacancy groups for clerical, technical and academic staff, with memberships of four, six and nine respectively.

B   Vacant chairs and readerships: referred to a committee specially constituted for each vacancy.

   More junior academic vacancies and non-academic vacancies: referred to a review committee comprising the Vice-Chancellor, two Pro-Vice-Chancellors, a former Pro-Vice-Chancellor and the Dean of Medicine.

C   Academic and non-academic vacancies: referred to a review group consisting of the Vice-Chancellor, the chairman of the Senate's development and estimates committee and the chairman of the Senate academic staff committee.

D   There is a separate committee for each of the undernoted categories of staff. These committees consider requests for filling of vacancies and make recommendations to the Committee of Deans.

Professorships
Non-professorial academic posts and non-professorial heads of
    departments
Clerical
Technical
Manual and ancillary
Administrative and academic-related

F   Academic vacancies: referred to a Faculty Vacancies group of the
    planning committee, consisting of the Vice-Chancellor, Pro-Vice-
    Chancellor and three ex officio academic members.

    Academic related vacancies: referred to a vacancies group consisting
    of the Vice-Chancellor, Pro-Vice-Chancellor, Librarian, Registrar
    and Finance Officer.

    Technical and secretarial vacancies: decisions are taken by the local
    equivalent of faculties.

I   Academic and non-academic vacancies: referred to three members of
    the resources committee (a lay member and two academic members).

J   Academic and non-academic vacancies: each faculty at its discretion
    may fill such vacancies, subject to meeting its savings target.

K   Academic and non-academic vacancies: referred to the budget sub-
    committee of the finance committee.

L   Academic vacancies: referred to a committee consisting of the
    Vice-Chancellor and the three Pro-Vice-Chancellors.

    Non-academic vacancies: referred to a Pro-Vice-Chancellor.

NOTES AND REFERENCES
1   Fielden, J. (1971) Management accounting in universities. In Shattock,
    M.L. (1971) *University Administration in a Period of Expansion*
    p. 58. British Council
2   Moodie, G.C. and Eustace, R.B. (1974) *Power and Authority in British
    Universities* p. 181. Allen and Unwin.
3   Sloman, A.E. (1964) *A University in the Making* p. 87. BBC
4   Dixon, M. (1982) How teachers learned a harsh lesson *Financial Times* 8
    September, p. 12

NORMS AND FORMULAE
IN DETERMINING ACADEMIC RESOURCE ALLOCATION

The academic budget covers expenditure under the following headings: academic departments, libraries, other academic services and general educational expenditure (see Table 2, p. 28). This chapter is concerned to examine the use of norms and formulae employed by universities in the process of resource allocation to academic departments for staffing (academic, technical and clerical) and consumables. Most norms or formulae were established to assist resource allocation in a period of expansion and to assist the distribution of new money. At least one large civic university, however, introduced a comprehensive system of norms in order to measure past maldistributions of resources so that over a period the university might find a way of bringing the distribution back into balance.

Norms and formulae have been widely used by universities in academic resource allocation. Sometimes they were introduced as a means of assessing claims submitted by departments, sometimes to provide a rational basis for de novo allocation. Universities say that they are rarely the final determinant of a decision in the academic resource allocation process, and resource allocating committees will generally balance statistical data of this kind with their own academic judgement. But the use of norms and formulae has a way of determining the shape of the allocation and can, if consistently applied over a period of years, have the effect of skewing resources in a particular way. The problem with norms and formulae can be that they are often invented to deal with particular circumstances but when the circumstances change it is difficult to persuade the beneficiaries to agree to their amendment.

Of course, norms and formulae can take the pain out of university decision-making and one of the new universities went so far in the early 1970s as adopting an overall student numbers-based package which had the effect of producing a virtually automatic allocation to departments. In fact, once the student targets had been fixed for the following year the allocation process was simply a matter of cranking a handle and the departments/schools were issued with their allocation. Significantly this process was brought to an abrupt halt in 1974/75 when, for the first time, the resources were no longer available to match the requirements projected by the norms. One result was the recasting of the university's resource allocation machinery to bring together student number planning and resource allocation in one committee with a combined Senate and Council representation. This new machinery, devised in the midst of the financial difficulties of the mid-1970s, appears to have stood the test of time and has coped effectively with the problems thrown up by the retrenchment of the 1980s.

A further important effect of establishing norms and formulae has been to open the decision-making process to scrutiny in academic departments. Almost invariably, when norms and formulae have been established they have been widely published in the university. There are many advantages to this. Most obviously it increases confidence in the resource allocation machinery but in addition it gives academic departments a settled baseline for their future planning and introduces some element of certainty into what can otherwise be an unstable environment for thinking about the implications of syllabus changes or changes in student mix.

STUDENT LOAD

Perhaps the best known quantitative measure for resource allocation is the staff/student ratio. In many ways, particularly in a period of financial stringency when the shape of the budget is susceptible to distortion by 'incremental drift', this is a less satisfactory measure than unit costs, but the staff/student ratio has become the dominant comparator between departments and institutions. To determine the student side of the ratio, student numbers have to be converted into 'loads', that is the proportion of each individual student which can be attributed to the teaching department concerned, bearing in mind that each individual student may be taught in more than one department. The approach to student loads varies widely between universities. At two of the universities a student taking physics, mathematics and management, for example, would simply be counted as one-third to each in spite of possible variations in teaching load between the three subjects. At another university the distribution of load is delegated to a grouping of subjects called an 'academic area' where a calculation based on proportionate teaching demands is used to distribute a 'block' grant from the resource allocation committee.

At one technological university 10% of a full-time equivalent (FTE) student is allocated automatically to the parent department (25% during the industrial year of a sandwich course) and the remaining 90% FTE is distributed among all the collaborating departments involved in the student's particular degree programme on the basis of teaching hours determined by course timetables. At another technological university each course syllabus is converted into a computer programme allowing for hours taught by collaborating schools and taking options and electives into account. The student load for each course, by year and optional selection, is then entered and the computer shares the FTE for each student among schools. The value of each student on a sandwich placement period is calculated as part of the exercise and added to the total load on the parent school of study. This 'sandwich element' is determined by a detailed costing exercise to allow for academic staff time during visits to the placement, travel, subsistence, the administrative cost of the arrangement and so on.[1] The university concerned argues that one of the merits of its approach is that it encourages economical teaching methods. Thus, if a class of 50 students visit the School of Chemistry for service teaching for 2 hours weekly and the students have a 20-hour week, the School of Chemistry is credited with:

$$50 \times (2/20) = 5 \text{ FTEs}$$

Within this formula the School has the freedom to devote 2 hours of staff time teaching the whole class of 50 simultaneously, or 10 hours teaching five classes of 10 students, without any change to the FTE load. This gives an inbuilt incentive to the economical organization of tuition patterns and prevents departments obtaining an advantage from the proliferation of options and electives. The method has been in operation for over 10 years and is sufficiently trusted for only the last line of the calculation of the load for each School to be published. An incidental advantage is that the computer programme will accept hypothetical populations of students and print out a resource allocation in terms of staff numbers, costs and space to suit. In effect, it is a resource model of the university, enabling the ready exploration of the resource consequences of change within the institution.

Another university sees its method as offering positive teaching advantages as well as a basis for resource allocation. In this university, which set out to encourage inter-disciplinary teaching and considerable student freedom of choice in selecting options, the student load is determined on the basis of a matrix derived from the course examinations which the student chooses to register for in March of each year. The precise loading is obtained from the examination 'weight' of the particular examination in the overall calculation of the student's examination marks. Students are encouraged to choose their options widely but they need only determine the courses they wish to be examined in at the end of their second term. Once again the method has been in operation for many years, in this case about fifteen, and the university clearly trusts it. A distinctive feature of the matrix is that it discounts any variations in teaching time on the basis of 'a student is a student is a student' wherever he may be found in the university. Some universities seek to attribute student load on the basis of the commitment of academic staff time but some limitation needs to be introduced in such cases to prevent over-teaching, or over-claiming. At one university adjustments are given to produce more than one FTE per full-time enrolled undergraduate when the commitment to the student lasts longer than the traditional academic year (eg 3rd and 4th-year students of the social work degree are weighted as 1.5 FTEs). Another university, which teaches sandwich courses, makes similar allowances so that a student can count for more or less than one FTE but the sum of School FTEs calculated in this way is then corrected to agree with the FTE load of the university.

POSTGRADUATE WEIGHTING

In the UGC's report *University Development 1962/67*[2] the UGC used 'weightings' of one FTE for all undergraduates, two FTEs for each arts-based postgraduate (other than PGCE students) and three FTEs for each science-based postgraduate for the purpose of estimating university costs. One result of this was that universities were encouraged to build up postgraduate numbers, and in some science subjects, where undergraduate numbers had fallen away, overall FTE numbers were maintained by the recruitment of postgraduates (counting three FTE) often of dubious quality. Many universities assumed that such weightings applied in the calculation of the recurrent grant. Sometime in the 1970s news filtered out of the UGC that postgraduate weighting was not used in this way for the purpose of recurrent grant allocation and since then many universities which had previously adopted weighting have sought either to reduce their weightings or give them up altogether. Of the universities studied three gave no weightings. Four, however, did as shown below:

TABLE 8

Postgraduate weightings in four universities 1979/80

Postgraduates	FTE weighting by university			
	A	B	C	D
Full-time				
Arts-based	1	1	1.25	1.5
Science-based	2	2	1.75	2
Exceptions to above				
Maths, geog. and management	1.5			
Chemistry and physics	2.5			
Education (research)		1.5		
Part-time	50% of the appropriate weightings			
Arts-based	0.63			
Science-based	0.88			

One university originally gave weightings as follows:

1st-year postgraduates in science and medicine	2
1st-year postgraduates in arts	1.5
2nd-year and 3rd-year postgraduates (excluding medicine)	1
Clinical medicine undergraduate and postgraduate course	1.6

| Clinical dentistry undergraduate and postgraduate course | 1.8 |
| All other undergraduates and DipEd | 1 |

But it has now abandoned differential weightings altogether.

Another, having moved from 1:2:3 to 1:1.25:1.75 has, rather than open Pandora's box by trying to convince its scientists, the chief beneficiaries of the weighting system, that weightings should be abandoned, chosen to publish staff/student ratios both on a weighted and an unweighted basis.

ACADEMIC POSTS

Staff/student ratios, particularly post July 1981, are rarely the final determinant in the allocation of a new academic post. All universities would argue that the variation within a university's departmental staff/student ratio shows that judgement is also involved. Sometimes such variations derive from allocations based on student weightings, sometimes on other factors. Some universities would add that they would expect experimental science departments to have a more favourable staff/student ratio than the rest of the university. One technological university accords priority for new posts when the ratio is 1: >11 and the automatic filling of vacancies when the ratio is 1:>10. If the ratio is 1:>9 and 1:>10, the post is frozen and/or disestablished until a new case is made. If the ratio is 1:<9 the post disappears.

Two universities have used regression analyses allowing for economy of scale although both reported that the use of regression was subordinated to judgement. One of these now reports that the analyses are abandoned and judgement is relied upon entirely. The other looks for a 10% deviation from the regression line as indicative that action is appropriate. The use of regression analysis is valuable in that it offers a method of compensating for economies of scale. The adoption of an arbitrary 10% 'trigger-for-action' level is questionable and appropriate for only two distinct population sizes. Regression analysis can support arguments based on equity but the adoption of a 10% threshold could result in considerable inequity. The choice of ± 10% may have resulted from misinterpretation and misapplication of the methods described by Pickford.[3] One large civic university relies heavily for its staff/student ratio norms on national averages by UGC subject heading in spite of the fact that they have generally been published some two years in arrears and that these figures represent the consolidation of a spectrum of very different circumstances.

The final GB average cost comparison column in Table 9 suggests that the overall staff/student ratio has little meaning without an acknowledgement of the exact mixture of disciplines.[4] It does not follow from the table that the more generously endowed institution in terms of the staff/student ratio is the most expensive in terms of cost.

For instance, university A has a generous staff/student ratio at 1:9.1 although its costs are low at 92%. University H has a ratio only slightly

TABLE 9
Staff/student ratios in nine universities and cost relationship with GB
average (excluding Oxford, Cambridge and London) 1978/79

University	Staff/student Ratios			Cost of GB average expenditure on academic staff
	Arts-based	Science-based	Overall	
	1:	1:	1:	%
A	10.9	8.4	9.1	92
B	10.5	8.2	9.8	102
C	11.5	7.9	9.0	101
D	11.5	7.3	9.1	102
E	9.8	9.3	9.4	104
F	10.0	7.7	9.1	97
G	10.9	7.8	9.0	99
H	10.5	8.0	9.0	107
I	12.5	9.0	10.9	86

better at 1:9.0 with its costs at 10% of the average for its mixture of
students. Is the average salary of a member of academic staff in university H
really better than that in university A by almost one-fifth? In fact the
real difference is that university H has 40% staff in senior grades whereas
university A has only 29%. Although the staff/student ratio may be roughly
indicative of the workload, the rewards for doing the work may be strikingly
different among institutions.

TECHNICAL STAFF
About half the universities surveyed relied on judgement alone, without
recourse to norms, for their allocation of technical staff posts. In the 1960s
the accepted norm for the ratio of technician to academic posts in science
departments was 1:1 but now, where universities use norms, the ratios
have become more sophisticated. One university, for example, has an
elaborate points-based system which takes the grade of the technical
appointment into account. Another with a subject area based system
arranges for the area committee to receive a block grant and to decide on the
distribution of funds (which are converted into manpower by division
by the average salary). The manpower is then divided one-third equally
among departments, one-third in proportion to academic posts and the final
third in proportion to FTE student and research staff numbers.

In general, points-based systems relate to sums of money. For example, in one university, biology, chemistry and physics each have an allocation of two points plus 0.91 points per academic staff member. The October 1978 value of a point was £4,227. It should be noted that a system of allocating points for each member of academic staff relies much on the department having the right number of academic staff. Any inadequacy in that respect would be compounded. It would operate very unfairly in one university where one department has a staff/student ratio of less than 70% of the GB average and another has a ratio which is more than 110% of the average. In that institution the technical establishment used to be points-based but for five years there has been an absolute moratorium on technical staff appointments and all available funds have been diverted to the improvement of the academic staff ratios. A sample of reported ratios is given in Table 10.

TABLE 10
Academic staff/technician ratios in science-based departments in eight universities and cost relationship with GB average (excluding Oxford, Cambridge and London) for all departmental support staff 1979/80

University	Academic staff/technician 1:	% of GB average cost for ALL dept. support staff
A	0.61	75
B	0.63	75
C	0.75	95
D	0.85	74
E	1.11	103
F	1.00	104
G	0.91	102
H	0.88	99

The final column in the table relates to technical plus clerical and administrative support staff expenditures as returned in Form 3. The pattern appears to be fairly consistent, except in the case of university D where the high ratio of technical to academic staff does not seem to accord with the low percentage of the GB average unless the other support staff at that university are very poorly paid.

CLERICAL AND SECRETARIAL STAFF
Six universities reported using a points-based or similar formula for the allocation of clerical and secretarial staff to departments. One university uses the formula:

$$N = (3/4)[(P/2) + (L/5)] + (S/200)$$

where: N = points P = professors L = other academics S = student load

In addition to the formula, various conditions are included about departments without professorial heads, personal chairs and so forth. The university stresses, however, that the formula is intended as an aid to the exercise of judgement and not as a replacement for it.

Another university allocates points as follows:

First FT teaching post	= 30 points
Next two teaching posts	= 15 points each
Next four teaching posts	= 10 points each
All others	= 5 points each
Each notional technician*	= 3 points

*Notional technicians are defined by another formula:
1 point = £70 based on salary levels at 1.7.1978

A sample of ratios is given in Table 11.

TABLE 11
Academic staff/clerical staff ratios in eight universities 1979/80

University	Arts-based, academic:clerical 1:	Science-based, academic:clerical 1:
A	0.21	0.15
B	0.17	0.18
C	0.19	0.28
D	0.20	0.20
E	0.18	0.22
F	0.19	0.22
G	0.20	0.20
H	0.23	0.19

In general the ratio is better in support of science departments than arts departments, with two notable exceptions, both of which are in technological universities.

DEPARTMENTAL EXPENSES
Three universities report that they made no use of formulae for determining departmental recurrent budgets. Last year's allocation is taken as the base-line, a factor for inflation applied and pleas for variation considered. In happier times, any free monies were shared among departments and then the total would be used as the base-line for the following year. One of these

universities is moving away from departmental requests on the basis that about 60% of a department's recurrent budget is made up of fixed-cost items and only 40% is flexible to allow for variation in student loads. One university granted an allowance per member of academic staff which at 1979/80 prices varied from £561 to £2,867 in accordance with agreed needs. These were, however, the exceptions.

Two other universities make an allocation per FTE which is increased annually to allow for inflation and only modified as a result of the presentation of special arguments. In one of these cases postgraduate researchers attract a separate departmental allowance as an inducement to the department to increase its research activities.

As examples of the use of formulae four cases are given below:

University A   The departmental running cost grant = (FTE student load + [Academic staff x 3]) x the (Group Unit Cost) and is scaled proportionately in relation to the total funds available. The Group Unit Cost is based on the average national unit costs for UGC subject groups but a decision is first made as to the appropriate group for any one department — eg some subjects classified by the UGC as social studies have a laboratory element in this university and a higher unit cost is considered appropriate.

University B   The sum available for science consumables is divided into two equal parts: one is allocated to Schools in proportion to the number of experimentalist undergraduates, the other in proportion to the total of teaching staff, experimentalist postgraduates and experimentalist research fellows.

University C   A two-part allowance as follows:

	Ratio		1978/79 value		
	Initial	Per teaching staff	Initial £	+	Per teaching staff £
Biology, chemistry, engineering, physics, drama studio	1.0	1.0	2,194	+	2,194
Psychology	1.0	0.5	2,194	+	1,097
Geography	0.65	0.5	1,426	+	1,097
Art, comparative studies, archaeology	0.65	0.16	1,426	+	351
All others	0.4	0.12	878	+	263

University D   A detailed paper listing each department separately is submitted for consideration, the departments being grouped and sub-totalled in UGC subject groupings. Various columns provide for each department:

1   Previous year's budget
2   Previous year's budget divided by departmental FTE
3   Value of orders committed but unpaid at year end
4   The extent of over or underspending at year end
5   Departmental FTE numbers for the previous 4 years
6   The departmental budget for previous year split as 60% fixed and 40% variable
7   The variable element expressed as £x per FTE

Provisional allocations are made and then when final FTE numbers are known, a final allocation is made.

COMPARATIVE DATA

We were interested to establish how far universities relied exclusively on their own assessments of need in resource allocation and how far they relied on comparative data about other universities. In the absence of any move by the UGC to publish its own norms, universities must inevitably rely for comparative data on an analysis of the UGC Form 3 returns and on the published tables in DES *Statistics of Education* Vol. 6.[5] With the demise of the annual six-volume *Statistics of Education* published by HMSO university statistics are now published by USR on behalf of UGC and a more speedy publication rate promised, but for the period covered by this study universities had to rely on a consolidation of UGC Form 3 returns circulated to Finance Officers some eighteen months after the end of the university financial year in question and the DES Volume 6 published some three years after the year in question.

University comments can be summarized as follows:

University A   Heads of departments make what deductions they can from *Statistics of Education* Volume 6, and are therefore exposed to the challenge that they are out of date. They also glean information about their peers from professional associations. Only the Vice-Chancellor and senior administrators are fully informed with available comparisons.

University B   Comparisons made only exceptionally — eg if there is significant and persistent overspending.

University C   Internal comparisons are made, and sometimes external comparisons, but not systematically.

University D	Comparisons are encouraged by the provision of as much information as possible.
University E	Comparisons are made for guidance but not for emulation.
University F	Comparisons are made but not as part of the budgetary process.
University G	Extensive comparisons are made.
University H	Internal and external comparisons are used by both plaintiffs and judges.
University I	Comparisons are made only occasionally but there is currently an exploration of opinions about the need for comparative data.
University J	Comparisons are seldom made and only rarely externally.

The responses are interesting because it is evident that such comparisons have an effect on resource allocation, whether or not the university admits to it. In those universities where widespread comparisons are made with other institutions, the levels of expenditure are very close to what would be judged to be average for their mixture of students. Those institutions where few such comparisons are made deviate much more from the average expenditure for their student loads.

One university undertakes a systematic and comprehensive statistical analysis of the 13,000 or so pieces of information collected by the UGC in Form 3 each year. With the data on computer file it is possible to compare each item of expenditure with its equivalent GB average expenditure in all other universities, weighted exactly for the student loads. The average (which excludes London, Oxford, Cambridge and the Business Schools) is determined by a regression analysis which therefore allows for any economy of scale. Confidence limits are also calculated so that a comparison of the actual unit cost within the institution with the average unit cost for the exact student load can be accompanied by a measure of the significance of the difference.[6]

Although the analysis tabulates unit costs for all expenditure heads in all universities and estimates an average unit cost for comparison, the results are most usefully tabulated as percentages. Tables 12 to 17 inclusive illustrate the percentage relationships with the GB average for a selection of types of British universities. Three large civics, one each of the smaller civics, and the new and the technological universities have been used.

Thus Table 12 illustrates the relativities of a large civic university in which the total weighted recurrent expenditure is estimated as 109% of what would be expected if they allocated resources at the British average

TABLE 12
Expenditure of a large civic university as percentage of average for GB
universities 1979/80

DEPARTMENTAL EXPENDITURE

	Academic and related salaries	Support staff salaries	Consumables and other expenditure	Total net expenditure
Education	61	41	44	57
Pre-clinical & dental studies	100	119	88	107
Clinical medicine	56	67	93	61
Clinical dentistry	82	144	118	92
Studies allied to health & med.	75	18	20	56
Engineering	120	170	183	138
Other technologies	0	0	0	0
Agriculture and forestry	0	0	0	0
Veterinary science	90	76	96	85
Biological sciences	107	130	155	119
Mathematics	135	111	129	131
Physical sciences	117	151	192	132
Business management studies	101	191	36	88
Social studies	83	101	123	86
Architecture and town planning	128	165	126	131
Prof. and vocational studies	0	0	0	0
Arts	105	86	120	104

NON-DEPARTMENTAL EXPENDITURE

LIBRARY EXPENDITURE
Salaries and Wages   101
Books   110
Periodicals   117
Binding   85
Operating costs etc.   61
TOTAL LIBRARIES   103

ACADEMIC SERVICES
Museums and observatories added
to totals
COMPUTERS
Salaries and wages   93
Payments to other universities 440
Other expenditure   37
Total expenditure   69
CENTRAL ED. TECHNOL.
Salaries and wages   103
Other expenditure   62
Total expenditure   97
OTHER ACADEMIC SERVICES
Salaries and wages   91
Other expenditure   65
Total expenditure   85
TOTAL ACADEMIC SERVICES   86

GENERAL EDUCATIONAL
EXPENDITURE
Examinations   120
Undergraduate prizes   106
Postgraduate prizes   233
Total prizes   202
Extra-mural classes   233
Vacation grants & field study 146
Other expenditure   363
TOTAL GENERAL EDUCATION   240

PREMISES EXPENDITURE
Rates   100
Rent   58
Insurance   137
Heat, water and power   114
Cleaning and custody   118
Ord. repairs & maintenance 133
Telephones   111
Other expenditure   0
TOTAL PREMISES   116

ADMINISTRATION & CENTRAL SERVICES
Salaries and wages   133
Other expenditure   133
TOTAL ADMIN. & C.S.   133

STAFF AND STUDENT FACILITIES
Careers advisory service   114
Grants to student socs.   197
Salaries of wardens   35
Deficits – inc/exp a/cs   70
Accommodation office   82
Univ. health service   93
Athletic facil., maintenance 141
Other expenditure   24
TOTAL STAFF & STUDENT FAC.   98

CAPITAL FROM INCOME   134

MISCELLANEOUS   105

TRANSFERS TO FURNITURE AND EQUIPMENT   75

TOTAL NET RECURRENT EXPENDITURE   111

ALLOCATIONS TO RESERVES   209

TOTAL WEIGHTED RECURRENT EXPENDITURE 109

TABLE 13
Expenditure of a second large civic university as percentage of average for GB universities 1979/80

DEPARTMENTAL EXPENDITURE

	Academic and related salaries	Support staff salaries	Consumables and other expenditure	Total net expenditure
Education	90	78	107	92
Pre-clinical & dental studies	84	82	118	88
Clinical medicine	116	123	128	119
Clinical dentistry	112	146	140	119
Studies allied to health & med.	0	0	0	0
Engineering	89	86	107	91
Other technologies	77	105	115	86
Agriculture and forestry	0	0	0	0
Veterinary science	0	0	0	0
Biological sciences	126	113	102	119
Mathematics	99	83	106	99
Physical sciences	118	110	108	117
Business management studies	103	153	38	100
Social studies	102	103	160	105
Architecture and town planning	200	350	86	217
Prof. and vocational studies	0	0	0	0
Arts	103	122	133	106

NON-DEPARTMENTAL EXPENDITURE

LIBRARY EXPENDITURE

Salaries and wages	78
Books	64
Periodicals	80
Binding	77
Operating costs etc.	48
TOTAL LIBRARIES	74

ACADEMIC SERVICES
Museums and observatories added to totals

COMPUTERS

Salaries and wages	46
Payments to other universities	200
Other expenditure	46
Total expenditure	47

CENTRAL ED. TECHNOL.

Salaries and wages	170
Other expenditure	117
Total expenditure	162

OTHER ACADEMIC SERVICES

Salaries and wages	140
Other expenditure	58
Total expenditure	120
TOTAL ACADEMIC SERVICES	68

GENERAL EDUCATIONAL EXPENDITURE

Examinations	68
Undergraduate prizes	0
Postgraduate prizes	107
Total prizes	79
Extra-mural classes	97
Vacation grants & field study	63
Other expenditure	45
TOTAL GENERAL EDUCATION	66

PREMISES EXPENDITURE

Rates	60
Rent	51
Insurance	68
Heat, water & power	109
Cleaning and custody	89
Ord. repairs & maintenance	85
Telephones	79
Other expenditure	0
TOTAL PREMISES	85

ADMINISTRATION & CENTRAL SERVICES

Salaries and wages	98
Other expenditure	99
TOTAL ADMIN. & C.S.	98

STAFF AND STUDENT FACILITIES

Careers advisory service	103
Grants to student socs.	34
Salaries of wardens	134
Deficits — inc/exp a/cs	147
Accommodation office	101
Univ. health service	155
Athletic facil., maintenance	44
Other expenditure	0
TOTAL STAFF & STUDENT FAC.	90

CAPITAL FROM INCOME	113
MISCELLANEOUS	169
TRANSFERS TO FURNITURE AND EQUIPMENT	0
TOTAL NET RECURRENT EXPENDITURE	92
ALLOCATIONS TO RESERVES	116
TOTAL WEIGHTED RECURRENT EXPENDITURE	96

TABLE 14
Expenditure of a third large civic university as percentage of average for GB universities 1979/80

DEPARTMENTAL EXPENDITURE

	Academic and related salaries	Support staff salaries	Consumables and other expenditure	Total net expenditure
Education	113	122	46	110
Pre-clinical & dental studies	109	124	81	112
Clinical medicine	91	56	76	80
Clinical dentistry	110	85	82	103
Studies allied to health & med.	101	100	77	99
Engineering	126	148	127	132
Other technologies	0	0	0	0
Agriculture and forestry	0	0	0	0
Veterinary science	0	0	0	0
Biological sciences	106	87	73	95
Mathematics	124	295	156	138
Physical sciences	121	153	144	134
Business management studies	0	0	0	0
Social studies	98	98	70	97
Architecture and town planning	139	110	72	132
Prof. and vocational studies	0	0	0	0
Arts	110	101	57	108

NON-DEPARTMENTAL EXPENDITURE

LIBRARY EXPENDITURE

Salaries and Wages	86
Books	174
Periodicals	95
Binding	124
Operating costs etc.	59
TOTAL LIBRARIES	103

ACADEMIC SERVICES

Museums and observatories added to totals

COMPUTERS

Salaries and wages	139
Payments to other universities	0
Other expenditure	192
Total expenditure	162

CENTRAL ED. TECHNOL.

Salaries and wages	134
Other expenditure	191
Total expenditure	142

OTHER ACADEMIC SERVICES

Salaries and wages	14
Other expenditure	87
Total expenditure	28
TOTAL ACADEMIC SERVICES	133

GENERAL EDUCATIONAL EXPENDITURE

Examinations	156
Undergraduate prizes	14
Postgraduate prizes	93
Total prizes	72
Extra-mural classes	115
Vacation grants & field study	94
Other expenditure	60
TOTAL GENERAL EDUCATION	90

PREMISES EXPENDITURE

Rates	84
Rent	83
Insurance	121
Heat, water & power	152
Cleaning and custody	91
Ord. repairs & maintenance	153
Telephones	94
Other expenditure	0
TOTAL PREMISES	121

ADMINISTRATION & CENTRAL SERVICES

Salaries and wages	111
Other expenditure	125
TOTAL ADMIN. & C.S.	115

STAFF AND STUDENT FACILITIES

Careers advisory service	131
Grants to student socs.	147
Salaries of wardens	82
Deficits – inc/exp a/cs	83
Accommodation office	126
Univ. health service	200
Athletic facil., maintenance	40
Other expenditure	0
Total expenditure	99

CAPITAL FROM INCOME	124
MISCELLANEOUS	61
TRANSFERS TO FURNITURE AND EQUIPMENT	57
TOTAL NET RECURRENT EXPENDITURE	107
ALLOCATIONS TO RESERVES	109
TOTAL WEIGHTED RECURRENT EXPENDITURE	110

TABLE 15
Expenditure of a smaller civic university as percentage of average for GB universities 1979/80

DEPARTMENTAL EXPENDITURE

	Academic and related salaries	Support staff salaries	Consumables and other expenditure	Total net expenditure
Education	78	78	159	85
Pre-clinical & dental studies	82	92	152	91
Clinical medicine	74	59	123	73
Clinical dentistry	0	0	0	0
Studies allied to health & med.	0	0	0	0
Engineering	93	141	73	104
Other technologies	0	0	0	0
Agriculture and forestry	0	0	0	0
Veterinary science	0	0	0	0
Biological sciences	110	142	157	125
Mathematics	121	559	418	125
Physical sciences	78	100	98	87
Business management studies	0	0	0	0
Social studies	101	98	103	100
Architecture and town planning	0	0	0	0
Prof. and vocational studies	47	93	102	55
Arts	88	82	79	87

NON-DEPARTMENTAL EXPENDITURE

LIBRARY EXPENDITURE

Salaries and Wages	131
Books	145
Periodicals	131
Binding	205
Operating costs etc.	126
TOTAL LIBRARIES	136

ACADEMIC SERVICES
Museums and observatories added to totals

COMPUTERS

Salaries and wages	86
Payments to other universities	61
Other expenditure	78
Total expenditure	82

CENTRAL ED. TECHNOL.

Salaries and wages	109
Other expenditure	33
Total expenditure	98

OTHER ACADEMIC SERVICES

Salaries and wages	21
Other expenditure	6
Total expenditure	18
TOTAL ACADEMIC SERVICES	105

GENERAL EDUCATIONAL EXPENDITURE

Examinations	123
Undergraduate prizes	8
Postgraduate prizes	23
Total prizes	20
Extra-mural classes	248
Vacation grants & field study	94
Other expenditure	69
TOTAL GENERAL EDUCATION	98

PREMISES EXPENDITURE

Rates	103
Rent	0
Insurance	92
Heat, water & power	98
Cleaning and custody	79
Ord. repairs & maintenance	89
Telephones	80
Other expenditure	3
TOTAL PREMISES	89

ADMINISTRATION & CENTRAL SERVICES

Salaries and wages	82
Other expenditure	99
TOTAL ADMIN. & C.S.	86

STAFF AND STUDENT FACILITIES

Careers advisory service	69
Grants to student socs.	110
Salaries of wardens	265
Deficits − inc/exp a/cs	29
Accommodation office	15
Univ. health service	120
Athletic facil., maintenance	49
Other expenditure	39
TOTAL STAFF & STUDENT FAC.	75

CAPITAL FROM INCOME	43
MISCELLANEOUS	40
TRANSFERS TO FURNITURE AND EQUIPMENT	0
TOTAL NET RECURRENT EXPENDITURE	92
ALLOCATIONS TO RESERVES	101
TOTAL WEIGHTED RECURRENT EXPENDITURE	90

TABLE 16
Expenditure of a new university as percentage of average for GB universities 1979/80

DEPARTMENTAL EXPENDITURE

	Academic and related salaries	Support staff salaries	Consumables and other expenditure	Total net expenditure
Education	142	121	131	134
Pre-clinical & dental studies	0	0	0	0
Clinical medicine	0	0	0	0
Clinical dentistry	0	0	0	0
Studies allied to health & med.	0	0	0	0
Engineering	90	103	88	93
Other technologies	0	0	0	0
Agriculture and forestry	0	0	0	0
Veterinary science	0	0	0	0
Biological sciences	79	78	286	103
Mathematics	70	60	142	72
Physical sciences	107	114	235	118
Business management studies	102	61	63	95
Social studies	103	67	100	100
Architecture and town planning	0	0	0	0
Prof. and vocational studies	0	0	0	0
Arts	86	64	91	85

NON-DEPARTMENTAL EXPENDITURE

LIBRARY EXPENDITURE

Salaries and wages	109
Books	133
Periodicals	41
Binding	157
Operating costs etc.	99
TOTAL LIBRARIES	103

ACADEMIC SERVICES
Museums and observatories added to totals

COMPUTERS

Salaries and wages	69
Payments to other universities	49
Other expenditure	66
Total expenditure	68

CENTRAL ED. TECHNOL.

Salaries and wages	157
Other expenditure	149
Total expenditure	156

OTHER ACADEMIC SERVICES

Salaries and wages	56
Other expenditure	48
Total expenditure	54
TOTAL ACADEMIC SERVICES	89

GENERAL EDUCATIONAL EXPENDITURE

Examinations	78
Undergraduate prizes	62
Postgraduate prizes	13
Total prizes	24
Extra-mural classes	1
Vacation grants & field study	67
Other expenditure	107
TOTAL GENERAL EDUCATION	64

PREMISES EXPENDITURE

Rates	109
Rent	0
Insurance	88
Heat, water & power	113
Cleaning and custody	163
Ord. repairs & maintenance	83
Telephones	108
Other expenditure	1
TOTAL PREMISES	112

ADMINISTRATION & CENTRAL SERVICES

Salaries and wages	91
Other expenditure	133
TOTAL ADMIN. & C.S.	102

STAFF AND STUDENT FACILITIES

Careers advisory service	95
Grants to student socs.	78
Salaries of wardens	4
Deficits – inc/exp a/cs	159
Accommodation office	89
Univ. health service	69
Athletic facil., maintenance	93
Other expenditure	200
TOTAL STAFF & STUDENT FAC.	100

CAPITAL FROM INCOME	304
MISCELLANEOUS	60
TRANSFERS TO FURNITURE AND EQUIPMENT	0
TOTAL NET RECURRENT EXPENDITURE	88
ALLOCATIONS TO RESERVES	10
TOTAL WEIGHTED RECURRENT EXPENDITURE	105

TABLE 17
Expenditure of a technological university as percentage of average for GB universities 1979/80

DEPARTMENTAL EXPENDITURE

	Academic and related salaries	Support staff salaries	Consumables and other expenditure	Total net expenditure
Education	94	7	15	31
Pre-clinical & dental studies	0	0	0	0
Clinical medicine	0	0	0	0
Clinical dentistry	0	0	0	0
Studies allied to health & med.	126	140	118	132
Engineering	119	99	95	111
Other technologies	134	163	131	137
Agriculture and forestry	0	0	0	0
Veterinary science	0	0	0	0
Biological sciences	97	93	74	92
Mathematics	96	77	76	97
Physical sciences	85	84	83	88
Business management studies	99	58	130	91
Social studies	112	94	86	108
Architecture and town planning	118	146	185	123
Prof. and vocational studies	93	187	58	101
Arts	108	85	62	104

NON-DEPARTMENTAL EXPENDITURE

LIBRARY EXPENDITURE

Salaries and wages	85
Books	69
Periodicals	79
Binding	43
Operating costs etc	24
TOTAL LIBRARIES	75

ACADEMIC SERVICES
Museums and observatories added to totals

COMPUTERS

Salaries and wages	88
Payments to other universities	159
Other expenditure	91
Total expenditure	90

CENTRAL ED. TECHNOL.

Salaries and wages	141
Other expenditure	229
Total expenditure	154

OTHER ACADEMIC SERVICES

Salaries and wages	82
Other expenditure	454
Total expenditure	159
TOTAL ACADEMIC SERVICES	90

GENERAL EDUCATIONAL EXPENDITURE

Examinations	69
Undergraduate prizes	36
Postgraduate prizes	61
Total prizes	55
Extra-mural classes	8
Vacation grants & field study	95
Other expenditure	42
TOTAL GENERAL EDUCATION	50

PREMISES EXPENDITURE

Rates	120
Rent	61
Insurance	77
Heat, water & power	62
Cleaning and custody	67
Ord. repairs & maintenance	87
Telephones	103
Other expenditure	0
TOTAL PREMISES	83

ADMINISTRATION & CENTRAL SERVICES

Salaries and wages	81
Other expenditure	78
TOTAL ADMIN. & C.S.	80

STAFF AND STUDENT FACILITIES

Careers advisory service	66
Grants to student socs.	10
Salaries of wardens	44
Deficits — inc/exp a/cs	0
Accommodation office	41
Univ. health service	29
Athletic facil., maintenance	93
Other expenditure	53
TOTAL STAFF & STUDENT FAC.	53

CAPITAL FROM INCOME	129
MISCELLANEOUS	80
TRANSFERS TO FURNITURE AND EQUIPMENT	0
TOTAL NET RECURRENT EXPENDITURE	89
ALLOCATIONS TO RESERVES	227
TOTAL WEIGHTED RECURRENT EXPENDITURE	94

level. Perhaps the most striking feature of the table is the size of the deviations from 100%. The relatively high cost of general educational expenditure and the high level of expenditure on administration and central services are particular examples.

Table 13 shows another large civic university with less significant variation than that illustrated in Table 14. Its total weighted recurrent expenditure is estimated as less than average and it may therefore feel subject to more restraint in its departures from the average. The 66% devoted to general educational expenditure contrasts with the 240% of Table 12.

Table 14 shows another large civic university, again with a generous total weighted recurrent expenditure at 110% of the GB average for its student load. Again there is a high level of variation and difference from the average distribution of resources.

Table 15 represents a smaller civic university, once again with a medical school, but in this case the total weighted recurrent expenditure is estimated at only 90% of the GB average for its size and mixture of students. Even more circumspection in the allocation of resources is suggested by the fact that no item of expenditure is significantly different from the variation of the peer group.

Table 16 shows a new university where spending seems to be exceptionally high on cleaning and security and exceptionally low on periodicals. We wondered whether there was a correlation.

Table 17 represents a technological university with an expenditure of only 94% of what could have been expected and yet with allocations to reserves that are exceptionally high. This perhaps suggests frugality elsewhere, particularly in expenditure on premises, general education and administration.

These tables illustrate perhaps more clearly than words that however much universities may have adopted norms and formulae to assist the judgemental process the result has not been to produce a conformity of approach. Whether the differences represent a variety based upon a genuine diversity of approach or merely represent an unreflective individuality is impossible to determine. What is clear however is that the differences are real and sometimes striking. They also demonstrate the degree of budgetary autonomy that universities are accorded through the block recurrent grant system. It must be expected that these differences will increase as a result of the financial stringencies imposed since 1979. Norms and formulae, at least in the university context, have tended to reflect a concept of relative stability in the system from year to year and it is a matter for conjecture whether universities which have had to jettison norms and formulae worked out before the cuts will devise new ones or will seek new ways of controlling expenditure.

NOTES AND REFERENCES

1 For more detail see Taylor, B.J.R. (1983) A cost basis for resource allocation for sandwich students *Proc. World Conference on Cooperative Education* 1, 384-389

2 *University Development 1962-67* (1968) Cmnd 3820, para 125. HMSO

3 Pickford, M. (1975) *University Expansion and Finance* p. 237. Sussex University Press

4 Weightings for the exact student load as in Taylor, B.J.R. (1982) Resource allocation in UK universities *The AIR Professional File* 11, 1-8

5 *DES Statistics of Education* Vol. 6 HMSO published annually

6 Taylor op. cit.

ACADEMIC SERVICES: UNIVERSITY LIBRARIES

Academic services consume just over 9% of universities' expenditure from General Income (see Table 3, p. 31). The single heading in UGC returns embraces libraries, museums and observatories, central computers, central educational technology units and a category described simply as 'other' which includes language centres, safety and radiation protection, industrial liaison, etc. Other than libraries, the largest of these services is computing, but computer services have special funding arrangements through earmarked grants from the Computer Board for Universities and from research councils. In addition, some universities house regional centres and others buy in services. Although some staffing is covered by the normal recurrent grant arrangements we decided that computer services were so intimately dependent on external funding that they did not warrant a separate examination in this study.

A more fruitful area might have been audio-visual and language services. Audio-visual services represented one of the great growth industries in universities in the late 1960s and the 1970s. The claim that teaching by television and other audio-visual services could produce economies in academic teaching has not in fact been substantiated, except in limited and particular areas. Certainly no university has found it possible consciously to worsen the overall staff/student ratio because of identifiable savings attributable to the audio-visual services. The case for the provision of such services now rests much more on their contribution to the improvement of the quality of teaching and on their particular use in certain subject areas. Against this universities must balance the cost of the services in terms of manpower, equipment and consumables, and it is perhaps not surprising that one effect of the UGC cuts has been a tendency for universities to make sharp economies in this area. This has probably been accelerated by the fact that audio-visual services are usually notoriously low in universities' political pecking orders, and in a time of acute financial stringency their main users are more likely to safeguard their own essential departmental interests than to risk further departmental economies by defending the audio-visual services from cuts. At one university a questionnaire issued to academic departments by the resource allocation committee elicited a clear response that, given the alternative, the departments would not sacrifice part of their allocation to maintain an audio-visual centre, however popular or respected its contribution. On the whole, language services have so far suffered less severely from the cuts, partly because their overall costs are much smaller, partly because their services are more directly integrated with the work of particular academic departments so that they have a strong constituency support, and partly because in some universities their role in attracting or retaining overseas students through programmes in English language teaching have been shown to have a positive financial contribution to make.

We have chosen not to make a detailed study of resource allocation to these audio-visual and language services because their costs nationally are not significant (though institutionally they can often be viewed as being extravagantly high) and because their size and importance within institutions is subject to considerable variation. Almost invariably the allocations are made by an academic committee rather than by a Council committee, and are subjected to rigorous and sometimes jealous scrutiny. The remaining categories of academic services are limited to one or two posts in any institution. Areas like safety and radiation protection are usually the subject of recommendations made direct by specialist safety committees to the finance committees of Council and the criteria on which the allocation of resources to them are judged are more likely to be pressures externally generated, such as safety legislation, than the availability of funds.

University libraries constitute by far the most significant item of expenditure under the general heading of academic services and present peculiar and special problems for resource allocation. Libraries represent a major academic facility, both as an adjunct to undergraduate teaching and a component in a university's provision for research. They therefore can make claims for resources based on both student numbers and on contribution to research. In addition they represent a kind of token of many of the basic ideals of a university summed up in the clichés about universities' roles as national resources for knowledge and expertise, as storehouses of learning and as repositories of scholarship. The library, more than any other part of the university, seems, not only to library staff, tangibly to embody the university's view of itself as having a place in society comparable to the medieval monastery. Library holdings are evidence that universities are permanent resource centres, not only for higher education but for society as a whole and for the community. The importance of the library can be seen in the invariable provision, even in universities with elected Senates, and unique amongst the academic services, of ex officio membership of Senate for the university Librarian, and in the respect and weight normally given to the views of the Senate's library committee as an apparently disinterested body. The university Librarian and the library committee can always call on an otherwise hidden constituency of academic and student support when cuts are being made, which is simply not available to the director of computer services, however relevant his services may be to the modern university. Support for the library in times of financial exigency is a kind of touchstone of one's belief in academic values.

It is perhaps not surprising, therefore, that resource allocation to libraries has resisted many attempts to introduce regulation by means of rational measures of book usage or other formulae. One of the greatest difficulties is that dependence on the library varies between subject areas. Obviously, arts-based subjects make greater book demands than science-based ones, but within these simple categories there are arguments for discrete and specialized provision for some subjects, eg law and medicine. Periodicals are of greater importance to the scientist, but are of such immediate and necessary use that he will want the most relevant to his field available within his own department. Student demand also varies to a considerable extent between subjects and between different times of the year. Intensive use of the library obviously occurs prior to examinations, which can introduce arguments for seating space as against space devoted to open shelves, which can lead on to arguments for staffing based on book stock retrieval, but more localized intensive use can occur as a result of timetables for the submission of assessed essays in departments.

Two further important factors are the presence of specialist collections and the geographical distribution of the library around a campus. Universities can acquire specialist collections either by the accident of gift or bequest or as the result of a policy to build up materials in a given area, because of particular strengths in the university or sometimes because of the characteristics of the university's neighbourhood. Such collections can be expensive to maintain and can require the outlay of non-recurrent financial support when complementary collections become available on the market. On the other hand, they confer prestige on the library and on the university and few librarians, vice-chancellors, or for that matter, Senates can resist having them. In theory they should support a flourishing research activity in the university and the far sighted academic planner might justify a major purchase by the likely attractiveness of a collection of bevies of future research students. In practice a sort of academic 'sod's law' seems to operate whereby research students who need the material seem rarely to be at the university where the collection is held and the member or group of academic staff around whose interests the collection is formed seem invariably to retire or move to posts in other universities by the time the collection has reached a significant size, leaving the university to maintain the collection on the off-chance that it will be of some internal relevance in the future.

The geographical distribution of the library, that is the dispersal of books into sub-libraries scattered round a university campus, is more often the result of historical accident than of locational needs. Examples can be found of large campuses concentrating resources in a central library and of smaller campuses having considerable devolution and dispersal. The academic advantages and disadvantages of either approach depend on subject, distance and external relationships (eg in respect of hospital services). As a rule of thumb one might have expected dispersed library systems to involve greater expenditure than centralized systems, partly because of their inability to make the economies of scale on the staffing side that would be open to a centralized system, and partly because of the additional pressure for expenditure from the academic departments benefiting directly from the dispersal. The figures quoted in Table 4 (p. 32), however, give no support to this, although this may reflect the difficulty of measuring costs on a proportionate basis to university expenditure as a whole rather than any true comparison of costs.

The most extensive study of university libraries was undertaken by a UGC established Committee on Libraries (the Parry Committee) which reported in 1967.[1] The Committee was established six months before the Robbins Committee reported and its report was published in the first year of a quinquennium (1967-1972) when the quinquennial settlement provided for a 10% increase in student unit costs. It suggested that 'the following criteria are among those which are important in determining the level of recurrent expenditure:

a   the number of subjects and branches of subjects in which teaching and research are carried on in the university;
b   the depth of research in each subject and the range of interests among the teaching staff — this is particularly applicable in disciplines where research is carried on by individuals rather than by teams, or where there is a departmental research programme;
c   the extent to which the topography of the university necessitates the establishment of outlying subject libraries, which usually involve duplication; and
d   special responsibilities, e.g. the existence of substantial special collections, collections of archives and manuscripts, and local responsibilities, for example to hospital authorities, agricultural research and to colleges of education.'[2]

These criteria were taken almost verbatim from a submission by the Standing Conference of National and University Librarians (SCONUL), as indeed was much else in the Committee's chapter on 'Finance'. SCONUL postulated a university of 3,000 undergraduates, 1,000 research students, 500 teaching staff, and an established library of 500,000 volumes in a single, modern, well-planned building, without inherited burdens such as old catalogues, congested buildings or older collections requiring servicing. Though not clearly stated, this model university did not teach medicine, dentistry or veterinary science.[3] Its annual acquisitions should be 16,000 books and 3,000 journals, requiring, with multiple copies and binding, an acquisitions budget of £98,000. A detailed schedule of the staff required was costed at some £60,000, giving a division between acquisitions and staff of 62½:37½. But in a later submission SCONUL denied that any such formula was intended, for probably no existing library conformed to the stated conditions. Without any further explanation, SCONUL stated that 'in present circumstances ... a ratio of 50:50, or even 45 (book grant): 55 (salaries) is probably more realistic.'[4] The 50:50 ratio pushed the budget of the model university library up to £200,000. The Parry Committee said that in view of the development of services to readers which it recommended the cost of staffing would inevitably rise and might even be greater than the cost of acquisitions. Rather simplistically, though correctly, it noted that a university of the size described might have a total annual budget of about £3,350,000, of which annual library expenditure of £200,000 would represent approximately 6%.[5]

The figure of 6% has gained an unwarranted status, probably never intended by the Committee, as a target aspired to by librarians. It is clearly questionable in several respects. First, a proportion of 25% research students was (and is) much too high. The actual percentage was under 10% in 1967, and even if *all* postgraduate students were meant the figure rises only to 17%. Secondly, the staff/student ratio, excluding medicine, dentistry and veterinary science, was 1:8.5, not 1:8, and is now a great deal worse. Thirdly, the model level of expenditure would be a different percentage of each university's expenditure depending on its circumstances. A university comprising 4,000 arts students can be expected to have a lower expenditure than a university comprising 4,000 science students because the latter has to bear the costs of laboratories, technical staff, consumables, etc. £200,000 would be a larger percentage of expenditure in the former than the latter. University expenditure patterns can be further distorted by non-UGC income, eg from research grants, from endowments, or for running major national facilities.

For all universities, the actual percentage between 1955-6 and 1964-5 was fairly constant, at around 3.8%. One effect of the Report was to raise it to 4.2% in 1971-2 and 4.4% in 1976-7 and 1977-8. But, probably because the acquisitions budget can be cut at short notice, the percentage had dropped to 4.1% in 1979-80. Our conclusion is that SCONUL's and the Parry Committee's model figures should be consigned firmly to history.

Although the Parry Committee was enjoined in its terms of reference to take into account the increasing capital cost of library accommodation, its consideration of capital costs is, in retrospect at least, remarkably slight. No planning norms of the floor area needed for each library activity are suggested. It is accepted that 'even in a numerically-static institution the library will, of course, continue to grow as more and more material of scholarly interest pours off the world's presses.'[6] Though it is acknowledged 'When considering essential growth in the next 25 years, that some withdrawal of material for deposit will have to be undertaken by university libraries,'[7] reference is only to *storage* away from the main library building and not to *disposal* of material by the library.

It was to the resulting inexorable demand for capital expenditure that a UGC working party addressed itself in 1975-76. The Atkinson Report on *Capital Provision for University Libraries* advanced the principle of 'the self-renewing library, of limited growth', in which new acquisitions will be offset to a considerable extent by withdrawals.[8] The principle was expressed in new norms on which the UGC could determine the needs of universities for library space provision. The previous norms allowed for the whole of a library's existing stock and anticipated accessions; the new norms included 3.8m² occupied shelf-space per FTE student, plus provision for that amount to expand by about a third over ten years on account of net surplus of acquisitions. Material withdrawn would go first into local stores and later to the British Library Lending Division which would dispose of material not needed for its own holdings. The Atkinson Report met with a predictably hostile reception from the universities; its norms are nevertheless the ones now published by the UGC, but the latter have been at pains to emphasize that the 'needs' as measured by the norms are only one factor in determining the building programme for libraries.

As Parry did not consider capital costs closely, so Atkinson did not consider recurrent costs closely, though he did acknowledge their existence. These were, in particular, the costs of selecting material for relegation and disposal (and of recalling it when needed), as against the combined capital and continuing running costs of extra accommodation and the cost of caring for 'dead' stock. The fact that the premises costs of the library are not separately identified in UGC Form 3 (but included under the general premises head) serves to obscure the trade-offs.

Thus if 'library expenditure' is confined to acquisitions and to the salaries of library staff, an increase in salary costs (and so in the proportion of library expenditure and of university expenditure on the library devoted to salaries) would be needed in the self-renewing library. But the demands on the premises budget would fall.

This is but one reason why Parry's proposition of a 50:50 split between acquisitions and salaries is now of little value. Others are that the capital and recurrent costs of computing for the library are now significant in many universities, but may or may not be carried on the library budget; that probably in the last fifteen years the rates of pay for library staff have increased faster than the costs of materials; and that the costs of materials are affected, as no other category of university expense, by fluctuations in foreign exchange rates.

None of the universities we studied seemed to have worked out a particularly effective way of judging their libraries' financial requirements agianst those of other academic areas. There seemed to be three main areas where practice varied: which body determined the library allocation, how it was determined, and the extent of discretion left to the Librarian in spending the allocation. In almost every case the library allocation was determined along with all other academic resources and not separately from them. The actual allocation was made by the main resource allocation body, in five cases by the finance committee of Council and in seven other cases by the Senate out of the block allocation handed down to it for academic purposes.

Most universities determined the size of the library allocation on the basis of the historic position, of assessed needs and of competition with other budgets. In two large civic universities (one not covered in detail by the study) the library has, however, effectively been given a first call on resources by being granted a fixed percentage of the UGC recurrent grant 'as locally defined', an important qualification bearing in mind the variations in the relationship between recurrent grant and fee income. In neither case has the library appeared to benefit disproportionately from this dispensation in the sense that their share of the universities' expenditure is in line with national averages rather than being in the region of the Parry 6% bench mark. Another university, one of the new universities, adopted a formula basis for allocation. The formula was devised to determine the year-to-year increase from the 1971-2 quinquennial base line to the 1976-7 target by calculating the planned increase in staff and students, giving them differential weightings, with further differentials according to subject area, to produce a number of 'reader units' which was divided into the planned increment in the budget over the quinquennium. The formula continued in use up to 1979 in spite of the collapse of the quinquennial system, and with the value of 'reader unit' index linked, when the termination of growth in student numbers and changes in the subject mix projected a decrease in allocation and caused its abandonment.

The critical major subdivisions of the library budget are between staffing and materials, and within the materials, between books, periodicals and 'other media'. Three of the universities studied have been sufficiently concerned about library expenditure generally that they have set up special working parties (in one case for the second time) to examine methods of resource allocation to libraries and have sought to protect the materials budget and to scrutinize the claims for expenditure on staffing. In one case at least the argument subsequently degenerated into a question of the curtailment of library opening hours. Several different methods are used to control the balance between staffing and materials. In two universities the finance committee determines the materials allocation but staffing bids are dealt with by another committee. In two universities the Senate library committee is responsible for determining the split. In a third the allocation discriminates between staff and materials but the library committee has powers of virement, while at a fourth a block allocation is made and the library committee is asked to recommend the split for the ultimate decision of the resource allocation committee. In one university the split is left to the university Librarian with, in some years, guidance from the finance committee on the staffing side. A further variation in one university is that the library may be given two allocations during the year, the first a basic allocation and the second, funded out of end-of-year surpluses, being restricted to book purchases. The second major split is between expenditure on books and on periodicals. Here an arts:science confrontation can occur and one university requires a fixed 40% of the materials budget to be spent on periodicals, with no periodical being able to be withdrawn without the threat to any individual title being discussed with the relevant department(s).

There is little consensus, however, about criteria for library allocations and most are based more on hunch than on well prepared data. The most difficult problem for any resource allocating committee is in penetrating the university Librarian's technical arguments to discover how far the management of the library can be streamlined. To do so can very easily be turned into an issue of confidence by the Librarian and can risk retaliation by the library committee, and an appeal to the wider constituency of library support at the Senate. For a university Librarian the most difficult feature in the management of his resources is that essentially he has to respond to demand. A syllabus change may intensify requirements in particular areas without warning, or the growing research interests of a particular research group may make special demands to which he feels he must respond. As his resources are reduced it becomes increasingly difficult to balance the demands on reader services with support for research. For the resource allocation committee the problem of library staff costs is now of acute concern but unless it can obtain independent advice on the internal management and staffing problems of a library it must rely on the Librarian's advice, and if it does not do so the university is at the mercy of the Librarian and the library committee in reducing opening hours or other services. Librarians understandably take the view that their professional expertise has a distinctive contribution to make on such issues and are in a position to pose technical difficulties which a committee finds difficulty in refuting. As with central administration (see Chapter 11) the difficulty of resource allocation is that in a period of expansion or modest contraction a committee does not have to face up to the detailed implications of its allocation, but when severe cuts are proposed it has difficulty in penetrating through the professionalism of the service to evaluate whether or not a cut of a particular size can be borne or whether a radical redistribution of allocation between staffing and materials is feasible.

NOTES AND REFERENCES
1 UGC (1967) *Report of the Committee on Libraries* HMSO
2 UGC op.cit. para 599
3 UGC op.cit. Appendix 8, p.266
4 UGC op.cit. Appendix 9, p.277
5 UGC op.cit. para 603
6 UGC op.cit. para 397
7 UGC op.cit. para 413
8 UGC (1976) *Capital Provision for University Libraries* Report of a UGC Working Party

RESEARCH

It is perhaps questionable whether in a study which sets out 'to examine the various main approaches adopted by UK universities to the allocation of their resources. ...' it is appropriate to give separate consideration to the policies, practices and procedures in regard to research activities of universities. After all, at the national level, because of the 'dual support system', with its 'comfortable confusion of teaching and research money',[1] there is no very clear picture of what resources are actually made available to the university system by government specifically for the support of research, as opposed to teaching or other activities; and lack of clarity at national level is mirrored at the institutional level, where the allocation of funds for research, except in very limited cases, does not constitute a separately identifiable process.

The 'dual support' system, which accounts for the universities' research funding from government sources, as opposed to funding for commissioned work from outside industry or through grants from private or charitable trusts, is seen as providing, through the UGC, a basic research 'floor', with its 'well found laboratories', this provision then being supplemented by secondary grants from the research councils, which make available the additional costs of specific projects. In fact, as the recent Merrison Report on the *Support of University Scientific Research* points out, the use of the phrase 'the well found laboratory' is an unhelpful piece of shorthand in that it obscures the full extent of internal university support for research. Merrison notes:

'The extent of the research infrastructure to be supported from general university funds is not always appreciated. It goes well beyond what is normally referred to as the 'well-found laboratory', and includes a proportion of salaries of academic, technical, secretarial and administrative staff, of library costs, and of computing and other services, in addition to the equipment, recurrent, and maintenance costs more commonly associated with laboratories; there is also the cost of the accommodation itself. In the social sciences administrative costs, and those of secretarial assistance, are of particular significance.'[2]

In addition to UGC and research council funds (deriving from the science budget allocated by the Advisory Board for Research Councils) further finance comes from the various government departments which received a transfer of resources, under the 1972 Rothschild reorganization, from ARC, MRC and NERC, and which, under the customer/contractor principle, commission specific research programmes directly from universities. Although statistical information about the amount of research council and government department funds granted to universities is readily available, difficulties arise when trying to assess the UGC contribution. The UGC itself does not identify that part of its grants, whether capital, recurrent, or for equipment, which is deemed to provide the research floor, and it issues no guidance to universities on this aspect of their funding. Various attempts have been made to assess this contribution, and a recent estimate by Merrison suggests that on average 30% of recurrent funds and 66% of equipment funds are devoted to research.[3]

This 'general accounting problem of identifying research expenditure' has been referred to in other recent studies, and the absence of appropriate data on which policies in regard to research can be based was severely criticized in the SRHE Leverhulme seminar on research.[4] In spite of the fact that ultimate responsibility for the funding of research in higher education comes under one department of Government, the DES, there appears to have been no serious attempt to take an overall view of policy, and therefore of funding, for research. It is, however, also surprising that in five of the universities looked at there was no focus provided within the committee structure for policy decisions on research, and that in two others such a focus had been found necessary only within the last two years although the average research income from external sources of these universities is in the region of 12% of their overall annual recurrent income, to which should presumably be added the Merrison calculation of 30% of general university income devoted to research support. On the other hand, it might be said that, since outside research funds are provided for a specific, previously identified purpose, there is no resource allocation decision to be taken. There may be a need to monitor the shape and direction of the academic development of the university's research, or to consider policy in regard to such matters as patent rights, royalties or commercial exploitation, but because of the project-specific nature of outside research funding, financing might be seen as following automatically on the successful award of a grant.

In fact, of course, the way the dual support system operates demonstrates the superficiality of such a view. First, a considerable amount of basic research activity is undertaken within the universities which does not attract outside support but is provided for from the university's general income. It is this essential work which in fact constitutes the 'initial and innovative investigations ... from which future growth points will emerge.'[5] Secondly, the UGC has calculated that the oncost on an external research grant or contract is on average in the region of 38-40%[6] and that, where a university does not include such an overhead in its grant application, it is in fact implicitly making a resource allocation decision. It needs, however, to be underlined that because the 'research floor' is deemed to be provided through the UGC grant, research councils and many charitable bodies do not, as a matter of policy, pay overheads. Thus, every grant of this type which is accepted is a charge on the university's other funds, and research council grants alone represent a very significant proportion of outside research monies. In 1979-80 in the universities studied, research council grants alone amounted to £20.53m, that is 56% of all grants and contracts (the figure for all universities being about 50%). This would indicate an overhead contribution from those thirteen universities from their own funds of £8.21m, that is **an average of £630K. It should furthermore be noted that** whilst the average percentage was 56%, in the newer universities in particular the percentage was much higher, ranging as high as 71%.

The CVCP drew attention to this implicit diversion of funds for research in the Report of the Steering Group on Commissioned Research Costs[7] in 1979, stating:

'Each grant of this kind represents an earmarking or diversion of some of the university's resources, and it is wise for the university to obtain, at least for a sample of cases, some appreciation of how large this diversion really is.'

A survey of the universities studied by the Group nevertheless revealed that none of them at present holds a formal record of its estimated contribution. In several cases administrative procedures provide for an assessment of the real cost to the university of a given application as compared to the costs actually being recovered, but in no case was there a further procedure to transfer such calculations either to a central, an area or a Faculty record, compiled in such a way as to give a realistic estimate of the picture as a whole.There is some evidence, however, that some universities are now reviewing their procedures in this area, and in particular their policies towards the recovery of overheads. The internal scrutiny which the current financial crisis in universities has forced upon them would seem to be bringing to the full consciousness of both administrators and academics a situation which they had been content to allow to remain dormant while funding overall was relatively generous.

Financial necessity may bring about some change of view, but the attitudes most commonly identified in relation to the financing of research tend to be based on a belief that research activity is not, and should not be, subject to institutional planning and control in the same way as, for example, undergraduate teaching; that it should develop naturally out of the strengths and initiatives of departments; and that excellence is more likely to be born out of a certain degree of anarchy. It is perhaps in the research area above all that the view that academic decision-making is best taken as close as possible to the point of action is most strongly expressed. This may explain the absence from many universities' committee structures of a research committee, and indeed, the procedures which universities have developed for the screening of research proposals before their acceptance, whether from the financial or academic point of view, tend to bear this out. Amongst the universities surveyed, the effective academic authority governing the submission of a grant application and its terms tended to be the head of the department concerned. In some cases a Dean or Pro-Vice-Chancellor, and in one case a Vice-Chancellor, was involved, but only in two cases did a central committee, with an overview of the university's research activity and senior academic representation, take part in the process. Administrative authority was particularly noticeable on the financial side — and the financial scrutiny was in most cases a technical matter of checking the accuracy of costings, rather than assessing any other more general implications. Only in the case of applications attracting overheads where a variation in the approved level was proposed did there tend to be an involvement of senior academics, either a Pro-Vice-Chancellor, or indeed in three cases, the Vice-Chancellor himself. In the majority of cases the Finance Officer or the Registrar, or in some cases an administrative officer at grade II or grade III level in a Faculty office acted to authorize the submission of the grant application and its eventual acceptance.

In the universities studied, practices in allocating the overheads recovered on research grants and contracts provide an interesting divergence of view. The overhead income could be seen as a resource which might be utilized to accomplish various ends. It might simply reimburse directly those areas of the university which have provided those services deemed to be covered by the overhead charge. On the other hand, it might be used as an incentive to the department or area generating the grant or contract in question to continue raising outside monies. Or again, it might be set aside in a special fund to promote research generally within the institution — or indeed to finance other specific purposes. No two universities took the same view on this question. At one extreme a smallish new university retained all overhead income for central university funds; another, a larger technologically based university, returned one third of the income to the department whilst putting the rest into a research and development fund, handling a budget in the region of £150K per annum which received bids from all areas of the university for university-financed research funding. In between these two extremes there were varying percentages allocated between central funds and departments/areas, with, on balance, the larger share going to central funds. In two cases a sliding scale was in operation which had the effect of giving the department/area a larger shareout the higher the negotiated overhead percentage.

It would be tempting to hypothesize as to whether there were any correlation between the type of institution, its organization, or its size, and the view taken about the allocation of overheads. It might have been thought that large universities with a faculty organization might have effectively engineered a greater return of the overhead income to the faculty, and that smaller, more centralized institutions would be in a stronger position to retain funds for the centre. Again, it might be thought that the older institutions with a longer research tradition and well established links with industrial contractors would have more sophisticated mechanisms for providing financial incentives to departments. However, a study of the various institutions concerned, and the type of procedure which they have adopted, does not throw up any significant pattern of this type.

Although a number of universities did not provide a focus for the discussion of general policy in the research area or the financial considerations pertaining to it in their committee structure, most universities set aside some funds to promote individual research projects which were usually administered by a committee set up for that specific purpose. The most common arrangement provided for a 'small grants' fund, to provide pump priming money to work up projects prior to an application to a foundation or research council, or to exercise a certain amount of positive discrimination in favour of those areas of the arts and social studies where outside funds were difficult to obtain. Usually the funds provided for an upper limit — in the region of £200-£300 — but on a couple of occasions rose to £5,000. Applications were usually from individuals, not departments. In the majority of cases the overall funds concerned were small — between £15K and £40K per annum, and only recently established, often from non-recurrent supplements to the UGC block grant. In one case, however, a fund with about £40K per annum gained its income from an appeal mounted for this purpose in the late 60s and early 70s, and in another, the only case where a substantial sum of money was available (£150K per annum), the source of income was the overheads from research grants, contracts and consultancies, plus the interest accruing from their investment.

Only in one case was a research fund used as an incentive or reward to departments already successful in attracting grants: an arrangement whereby in one university a small sum — £20K — was set aside each year from the UGC recurrent grant, and allocated to departments in proportion to the amount of money they raised the previous year from the research councils.

Although these funds do indicate a certain interest on the part of institutions in taking positive action at the institutional level to promote and direct research, it should of course be borne in mind that the funds made available are in almost all cases extremely small in comparison to the overall research expenditure of the institution, which has not in general been considered as an appropriate area for strict institutional control. In this connection, however, and given the present general absence from the financial decision-making structures of committees charged with responsibilities in regard to research, it will be interesting to assess the response of the universities to one of the major recommendations of the Merrison Report, which is that the universities should take measures to direct more funds towards research from within the overall funds available to them, that they should do so selectively, and that they should therefore consider the establishment of mechanisms and administrative processes to enable them to do so. The mechanism identified as most appropriate is the research committee, which would be charged with reviewing areas of research in the university and discussing their relative strengths, and would then have the responsibility of ensuring that, in the internal allocation process, the areas agreed received adequate funds for research along the lines normally associated with the UGC side of the dual support system.[8]

A necessary corollary of the introduction of research committees with this type of function would of course be the development of management information systems which would provide financial and statistical data to enable the university to assess and monitor its actual expenditure on research, and also of performance indicators to assist in the assessment of those high quality areas worthy of particular support. Evidence from those universities studied, and indeed from Merrison, is that present procedures whether at institutional or national level are not adequate to the task.

It appears that most universities have allowed their research activity to develop at the departmental level without very much intervention from the centre: and their committee structures, practices and procedures have reflected this. The financing of the major research effort has not been seen as a separate part of the internal allocation process, but as provided for in the main by external project specific funds, reflecting the philosophy of the dual support system. However, whilst such an attitude has been workable in the past, with university funds sufficient to provide the necessary back-up, the declining resources now available focus the minds of hard pressed chairmen of departments and administrators alike, who increasingly find themselves embarrased by the heavy demands in terms of accommodation, equipment, technical and secretarial support, which the acceptance of a major research grant can entail. Moreover, once finance becomes constrained, attitudes to the internal distribution of income recovered through overheads begin to harden and conflicting interests begin to make claims. Against this background, whatever the view in an institution as to the conditions most conducive to the promotion of excellence in research, to the presence or absence of control, or to the need or otherwise for incentives, it would seem essential that management information should be available in such a form as to allow the institution to assess the level of its activity and the cost of that activity in terms of the actual use of resources which it entails.

In other words, the harsh realities of the financial climate of the 80s may now dictate an explicit recognition of an implicit process of resource allocation which the more favourable conditions of the 60s and 70s served to obscure.

NOTES AND REFERENCES
1 The research jungle *THES* Editorial 19 March 1982
2 Merrison Report (1982) *Report of a Joint Working Party on the Support of University Research* Cmnd 8567, p.6, para 4 HMSO
3 Merrison Report op.cit. p.23, para 29
4 Oldham, G. (Editor) (1982) *The Future of Research* pp. 82-149 and 211. SRHE
5 Merrison Report op.cit. p.6 para 6.
6 UGC Letter of Guidance dated August 1971. Supplementary to *UGC Notes for Guidance to Universities on Charges to Outside Bodies for Work Done on their Behalf* February 1970
7 CVCP Commissioned Research Costs Study: (Circular VC/77/157), 1 December 1977
8 Merrison Report op.cit. p.28

THE EQUIPMENT GRANT

In 1968-9 the UGC introduced a new system for financing the purchase of equipment for teaching and research. Prior to the introduction of the new system there were two ways in which UGC funds could be used. The first was to call on the normal recurrent block grant, which was the only UGC money that could be used for replacing or augmenting equipment in existing buildings. The second was to tap the non-recurrent grants which the UGC made for furnishing and equipping new or existing accommodation being brought into new use. These latter grants were related specifically to the initial equipment required for particular building projects, and were not available for the purchase of equipment for existing buildings.

These arrangements were not satisfactory. The restriction on non-recurrent grants for new buildings meant that departments which were not moving into new accommodation often could not get funds from the university's recurrent income to deal with renewal and replacement or for new developments. The system therefore tended to lead to disparities between universities which had large building programmes and those which had not, and between departments which had new buildings coming into use and those which had not. The distribution of the resources available for equipment tended to be determined by building programme considerations instead of being related to equipment needs based on teaching and research programmes. Replacement of existing equipment in existing buildings was becoming a problem in the late 1960s and was to become an even greater problem in the 1970s.

The new system of equipment grants introduced by the UGC for 1968-9 took the form of annual block sums of money paid to each university in monthly instalments and assessed for a number of years in advance. The quinquennial system of funding was still operative and the grant announcements were intended to coincide with other planning arrangements. The basis of the assessment was, in the main, the planned student numbers in each university, with appropriate weightings to allow for differences in the faculty mix and for differences in the proportion of postgraduate and undergraduate students. In particular cases these basic grants were supplemented by additional sums to meet requirements which could not be related to student numbers, for example in new universities, or where justified by major new academic developments such as the establishment of a wholly new department or school. The new grants were made specifically for the purchase of equipment but the spending of the money was entirely in the hands of individual universities. It was for them to allocate it between departments which were moving into new buildings and those which needed to re-equip existing buildings. The new procedure applied only to the provision of equipment for teaching and research, including audio-visual aids and office machinery used in academic departments. Furniture, together with equipment required for non-academic purposes, continued to be dealt with in the old way by non-recurrent grants for the cost of the initial furnishing of new or adapted premises and recurrent grants for the replacement of furniture and non-academic equipment.

With effect from 1972-3 an 'indicated' sum was added to the equipment grant to cover furnishings in new buildings. From 1973-4 onwards the grants have also included amounts to cover the cost of repairing and replacing existing furniture, covered previously in the recurrent grant. Specific furniture grants for large new buildings, however, have continued to be made. The UGC announcement of the furniture and equipment grant is usually made in conjunction with the recurrent grant. Universities may supplement their equipment grant by making additional allocations from their general recurrent income.

Very few universities, however, appear to do this on a regular basis, although non-recurrent allocations to meet cases of specific need are not uncommon.

The division of the total funds available between furniture and equipment is largely at the discretion of individual universities, although where replacement furniture is to be funded entirely from the grant the UGC normally indicates an upper limit on the expenditure. Since 1979-80 the UGC has recommended that furniture expenditure should be less than 7% of the total grant. This is not a mandatory ruling but is a guide as to how the grant should be divided. Indications show that about a half of the universities studied have elected to follow the recommendation. There is no pattern to the reasons given for not doing so other than the particular needs of the situation.

In most universities the finance committee of Council is involved in deciding the initial division of the grant between furniture and equipment. Thereafter, the actual allocation of equipment funds to departments is generally carried out by an equipment committee or some other form of sub-committee reporting to the finance committee. In the majority of cases these allocations are treated as recommendations which require a formal approval by Council. Normally this is done through the finance committee but some universities require a report to Senate (through an academic planning or development committee) before reaching Council. Only one university was found to have no formal structure for allocating the equipment grant and in that particular case the Vice-Chancellor considers requests and allocates according to need. There appears to be no more consistency of practice in the structure of the committees than in their constitutional processes. Membership can vary from as few as two academic members and the Finance Officer to as many as three Pro-Vice-Chancellors, four Deans, the Librarian and four other members of the academic staff. In almost half of the universities studied the Vice-Chancellor was an active member of the allocating committee.

With the establishment of the equipment grant system in 1968, the UGC indicated that it would be left to individual universities to arrange the procedures for the allocation of grants to individual departments and for the control of expenditure. It is clear that each university has adopted an individual approach to the allocation process. There is, nevertheless, a good deal of common ground between universities, and the methods of allocation generally fall into one, or a mixture of, the following:

1   *On the basis of formulae*
    The formulae vary considerably from university to university but many contain common elements. One university bases its allocation on past allocations combined with a ten-year depreciation factor. It estimates and updates to current price levels the allocations to the science departments in the period 1967-72 (themselves related to 1962-67) and grants a notional replacement rate of 55%, while allocating £3 per unweighted student to non-science departments. Another uses the following formula as a first guideline: 25% on the existing UGC financed departmental inventories, 25% on the last three years allocations, and 50% based on student load weighted 9:1 science to arts-based subjects. This university then considers each case on its merits against the figures provided by the formula. A third university takes the formula basis even further. Having taken an allocation for maintenance and rental of the central computing laboratory off the top, it places 20% into a reserve fund. The remainder is allocated 80% to a named list of category A departments and 20% to a B list. The A list figure is then allocated on a student number basis while the B list is allocated on the basis of a fixed percentage of the sum available to B list departments, eg economics 1.8%, audio-visual 3.9%, etc. Departments submit separate bids for the reserve fund which is, however, allocated against need on the original 80/20 basis between A list and B list departments.

2   *On the basis of stated need*
    Four universities use no norms or formulae at all. In one case the whole exercise is carried out by the Vice-Chancellor himself. In another, equipment is allocated to science departments on the basis of £x per member of staff but no bids are invited from non-science departments and requests are dealt with ad hoc. Small equipment requests from non-science departments are dealt with by the Finance Officer.

    Where 'need' or sometimes 'merit' is said to be the basic criterion for allocation, and where norms or formulae play no part in the process, the decision-making machinery is that much more important. In one case equipment was handled by a departmental grants committee of the finance committee, a body which also allocates funds for consumables, stationery and other departmental expenditure, but in other cases the committee which made the recommendation to finance committee was sui generis and not connected with the main academic planning/resource allocation procedure. In one case the university had recently reviewed an unwieldy committee made up of the heads of science departments under a neutral chairman and replaced it by a three-man committee which allocated 40% of the grant on an ad hoc basis to meet routine requirements, and 60% on merit for the purchase of major items.

3 *Loan*
Where departments require exceptionally expensive pieces of equipment, some universities have introduced an internal loan scheme whereby departments can spread the cost over a number of years by committing some of the grant they will receive in future years. This method overcomes the necessity for departments to build up balances before they can purchase equipment, a practice which the UGC suggests should be avoided. In some ways this is merely a variation on the policy of over-commitment which is considered below.

In 1968, when equipment grants were first introduced, it was envisaged that universities would no longer need to draw on their normal recurrent grant to meet the equipment needs of existing buildings. In practice the flow of resources went the other way and as pressure grew on the recurrent grant, and as the need for equipment spread to arts and social science areas, so there developed a tendency to seek to charge items to the equipment grant rather than to the normal recurrent grant income. The UGC guidelines relating to the general utilization of equipment monies, which are defined in its *Notes on Procedure*, allowed a limited flexibility and within these limitations the annual grant for equipment could be used at the discretion of individual universities. The restrictions imposed by the UGC, which were last amended and published in full in 1977, have shown a general relaxation over the years to allow a greater degree of flexibility. This has been particularly helpful in redefining some items which could be charged against equipment funds and in the more general use of recurrent funds for equipment purposes.

Probably the most significant change in items of expenditure which may be charged against equipment funds was introduced in 1971 when the UGC agreed to allow the cost of maintenance contracts with outside firms to be a charge against either recurrent or equipment funds. With such large sums involved this made a considerable improvement in flexibility and several universities are responding to the contraction of the recurrent grant by transferring equipment maintenance costs wholly to the equipment grant.

The extent to which the recurrent grant can now be used for equipment purposes has also provided a very welcome improvement in the overall utilization and control of financial resources. When the equipment grant was first introduced, the UGC would only approve the use of general income for equipment to a very limited degree, such as meeting some special or unforeseen need. Since 1977, however, when the revised *Notes on Procedure* stated that there was no formal restriction on the use of recurrent grant for equipment, universities appear to have received every encouragement to use the flexibility arrangements in this area to their fullest extent.

While universities generally welcome the freedom in the use of resources which this flexibility provides, there remains the problem that, since the equipment grant has fallen by about 30% in real terms in the 1970s, the main contribution of the flexibility arrangements is to permit a certain amount of 'teaming and ladling' within a reduced income. About half of the universities studied obviously feel that equipment needs fully utilize the equipment grant and they do not allow other items, such as outside maintenance costs, to be charged against it. The other universities allow a degree of flexibility at departmental level within the UGC rules (outside maintenance contracts, etc.) and in some cases transfers of allocated funds between equipment and departmental grants are approved, but only when a matching request can be made for transfers in the opposite direction.

Prior to 1974 the furniture and equipment grant was paid direct to universities in monthly instalments in the same way as the recurrent grant. However, in order to avoid the build-up of credit balances within universities, which was the cause of critical comment by the Comptroller and Auditor General, the UGC decided to change the system, so that the monthly instalments would be first placed to the credit of a deposit account with HM Paymaster General. The amount in the deposit account would be regarded as belonging to the university, and could be carried forward from year to year. However, the university receives no interest on the accumulated balances. When a university's total cash balances, whether held centrally or departmentally, are less than one month's grant (at the current rate for the academic year in question) the university may apply to the UGC for a further payment which, provided it does not go beyond the amount standing in the deposit account, will be calculated to top up the university's balance to the equivalent of three months' grant. If purchases justify it at any time, additional grant may be claimed up to the limit of the university's credit in the deposit account.

The problem of substantial credit balances, which had resulted in the changed system described above, continues to persist, even though the balances are now largely held by HM Paymaster General. This reluctance by universities to commit equipment funds was not encouraged by changes in the funding arrangements introduced by the UGC. Both the abandoning of the quinquennial system, which removed the long-term planning base upon which universities could rely, and the delay in the announcement of the annual grant created an element of uncertainty regarding the future expectation of equipment funds.

In 1979 the UGC wrote to universities advising them of the effect that such balances might have on the enhancement of the equipment grant in the future. In order to overcome the problem they were asked to consider the following with regard to its allocation and spending:

1 Timing allocations to departments to ensure speedy acquisition of equipment and payment for it. Attention was drawn to a possible need for some universities to pay closer attention to the implications of the time-lag between the ordering and delivery of equipment; some system of notional 'over-commitment' could be a means of avoiding a backlog in payments, provided that it could be timed to avoid overspending.
2 Improving inventory keeping so that a university might acquire accurate knowledge of the current and likely future equipment situation within its departments.
3 Making a periodic review during the year.

The majority of universities have taken positive steps in answer to the UGC's appeal but there seems to be little uniformity in their approach to over-commitment. Of the universities studied, only three had set a specific amount of a percentage of the grant aside as a ceiling for over-commitment but even here this has generally been set at a fairly low level. About one-third of the universities actively encouraged departments to anticipate future grants and commit funds as soon as practicable but this had rarely led to over-commitment. It is, perhaps, too early to judge the effect of the over-commitment policy as a way of reducing cash balances held by HM Paymaster General and the universities, but initial impressions are not particularly encouraging. At the end of the 1979-80 financial year almost one half of those providing information showed balances in excess of 30% of the total equipment and furniture grant. The only conclusion that can be drawn from this is that universities have tended to be over cautious in their approach to over-commitment or find considerable difficulty in estimating the time-lag between the ordering of and the payment for goods and services. To find the correct balance between over-commitment and cash balances is not an easy process and may ultimately be achieved only by trial and error over an extended period of time.

The revised equipment grant system appears substantially to have met the original UGC objective of providing specific funds for the renewal and replacement of equipment in existing buildings as well as providing equipment for new developments, and with the passage of time, changes have been introduced most of which seem designed to enable universities to supplement the grant from recurrent income. The new flexibility appears to have been generally welcomed in universities. One of the main difficulties it seems to have created for the UGC is in the presentation of reliable statistical information. Universities are required to show in the UGC Form 3 returns any supplementary contributions made to the equipment fund from recurrent resources. However under the flexibility provisions large sums which can be charged to either recurrent funds or equipment grant need not be identified. Thus a university which charges outside maintenance contracts to the equipment fund may, in addition, show in its Form 3 return a supplementary allocation from general recurrent income. On the other hand, a university may charge outside maintenance contracts against general recurrent income and decide not to make any supplementary allocations. From returns made to the UGC the impression would be given that one university had made additional funds available for equipment purposes and the other had not. In essence they would be exactly the same but the UGC would have a very distorted picture.

Over-commitment has been encouraged by the UGC for some time and to a limited degree seems to have been accepted by universities. However, over-commitment can create cash flow problems if not exercised with some discretion. The UGC normally pays the equipment grant to universities (via HM Paymaster General) on a monthly instalment basis. There is, therefore, always a danger, particularly in the early months of the financial year, that universities will spend more than the UGC has made available. This would probably lead to equipment funds being charged with interest on overspent balances. The possibility of an adverse cash flow has made most universities very cautious in their approach to over-commitment and consideration should be given to revising the method of paying the equipment grant.

If the UGC needs to rethink its procedures it is probable that the universities need to as well. The difficulty about allocating the grant within universities is that different subjects have very different needs and very different capacities for obtaining particular pieces of equipment from other sources. Some subjects fall more easily within research council committee structures than others and within any institution some departments will simply have a better research track record than others and therefore be more likely to obtain the required equipment from external sources.Thus, in addition to the teaching requirements of a department, research needs must also be borne in mind. Equipment committees therefore need to be sensitive, not only to the policies of research councils and other grant awarding bodies, but also to the real needs of departments and individuals. Because so much of the equipment grant is committed to science departments, the criteria for allocation is often obscure to their art-based colleagues, and the principles of allocation are rarely discussed outside the committee itself or the science faculty. This is unfortunate because there are real dangers that important academic decisions will be locked away in equipment committees where the 'robber baron' mentality is more likely to dominate than in any other resource allocating committee in the university.

10

BUILDINGS, MINOR WORKS, MAINTENANCE AND SPACE

The subjects of this chapter, which may be given the single label of
'premises', encompass three distinct aspects of resource allocation, the
allocation of funds for the purchase or construction of buildings, roads,
gardens, etc.; the allocation of funds for the operation, maintenance and
modification of these capital assets; and the allocation of the use of those
assets by component parts of the university. The usual shorthand terms
for these three aspects are 'capital development' 'maintenance of premises
and minor works' and 'space allocation'.

The terms of reference and composition of the senior committee
responsible for the premises budget and the general mode of its handling,
show considerable uniformity among the universities surveyed. Greater
diversity is apparent in relation to other elements of the universities' budgets,
and the uniformity may owe something to the common body of procedure
followed for capital development. Invariably the responsible body is a
buildings committee, reporting directly to the university Council, although
one university changed to this arrangement only in 1981.

But within that uniformity there is diversity of detail. The most common
arrangement is that the buildings committee (or, for example, site
development board or development committee) has between ten and twenty
members, of whom the majority are academic, but has a layman in the
chair who is also a member of the Council. The committee is responsible
for all three functions identified in the first paragraph and works through
two, three or four sub-committees which often follow the same functional
divisions. In some universities there are two Council committees, one for
capital development, minor works and space allocation, and the other for
maintenance and services; there seems now to be a move towards
amalgamating these. In one university the changed financial situation
prompted the committee to abolish the maintenance sub-committee
altogether, in spite of the savings it obtained by scrutinizing the overall
estimate. In two other universities maintenance and services activities are not
under the specific control of a committee, and the budgets are fixed through
the finance committee and remitted direct to the appropriate administrators.
The committee structure of one very large civic university is *sui generis* and
is so different from others that it is presented here in a diagram (Figure 15).
It is particularly interesting because of the responsibility given to the Senate
sector. The university particularly stresses the fact that the physical development plan should be regarded as 'the handmaiden' of academic need.

FIGURE 15
Committee structure for consideration of matters relating to premises in a
large civic university

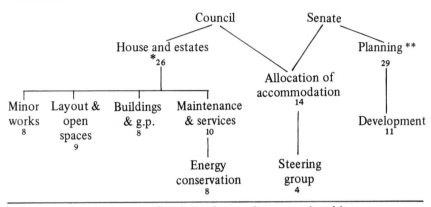

* The numbers represent the sizes of committee membership
**Function not confined to building development

CAPITAL DEVELOPMENT

Only very small proportions of the universities' building stock other than
student residences, except in two of the technological universities, are
rented, or acquired with loans which have to be serviced and repaid in later
years. Rather, the great majority of buildings currently occupied by
universities were funded by outright grants from the UGC and from external
donors, and are debt-free assets of which the individual university is the
owner. Hence the cost of construction, or the value of the building
represented by rent, is not of itself an element in the university's recurrent
budget. Land and buildings generally appear in university balance sheets at
historic cost.

Capital expenditure by the UGC on university sites and buildings was
at an unprecedented level for sixteen years between 1957 and 1973/4.
The peak for allocations to building starts was 1964/65, at £50.6m[1] (about
£340m at 1980/81 prices), in which year £9.6m[2] (excluding minor works)
was allocated. The expenditure of such large sums of public money by
non-government and non-statutory bodies led to the establishment of an
elaborate system of control by the UGC. Contracting procedures were
scrutinized in the reports of committees chaired by Sir George Gater
(1956)[3] and Sir Arthur Rucker (1960).[4] The procedures to be followed by
universities for grants payable by the UGC were set down in successive
editions of *Notes on Procedure: Capital Grants.*[5] The 1974 edition
incorporated the system of capacity planning intended to handle a period
of major university expansion now in abeyance.

We have not looked in any detail at the universities' procedures for allocating funds to capital development, for the purchase and construction of buildings, mainly because the period of major capital development is now past and there is little likelihood that it will recur in this century, for demographic no less than financial reasons. Since the UGC became the major source of capital finance, a university has not normally been faced with the problem of allocating money between projects (except by way of topping up) because the UGC's grants were earmarked for specific projects. A university exercised its choice as between projects when it put certain ones forward for inclusion in the UGC's building programme, and that choice formed part of processes concerned with the university's general planning and with the development of its site. It would be of some interest to examine the processes by which universities arrived at their stated priorities for new buildings as submitted to the UGC, though this information would be of limited value without corresponding information as to how the UGC determined the national building programme. Successive government statements have indicated the projections which have led to overprovision of buildings in particular disciplines. At the institutional level, even in the new universities, academic and physical planning may have been insufficiently integrated. It was assumed that all disciplines would grow, and the programme may have been determined by the comparative degree of inadequacy of each department's existing accommodation rather than by a detailed planning process. This has left most universities with some uncomfortable problems, since the stock of buildings does not correspond to today's needs and there is no easy way of remedying the imbalance.

Since this study began, the situation has changed. With effect from April 1981, only projects costing over £1m are included in the UGC's building programme and assisted by earmarked grants, and universities are free to finance projects up to £1m from their general income. The previous limit for projects financed from general income was £100,000, which will buy a small extension to a building. But £1m is enough to build 2,000 sq.m., which represents academic space for 800 undergraduates in arts subjects not requiring specialist facilities. Furthermore, even if the expenditure is spread over the two or three financial years over which the contract runs, finding £1m from within the university's annual budget may make the choice between capital and recurrent expenditure a difficult and controversial matter. But the money which was previously allocated through the UGC's building programme to projects between £100,000 and £1m has been allocated to universities in 1981/82 in the form of earmarked grants for capital building works generally. It may well be that earmarking will continue and the distribution will allow for agreed medium-sized projects, so that new arrangements will entail only removal of the detailed controls on design and contracting associated with projects in the building programme, and will not pitch capital into competition with recurrent expenditure in the university's budgetary process. Removal of such controls has been part of the 1979 Conservative Government's programme to reduce the size of the Civil Service and was probably the starting point for the new arrangements. It is too early to say whether consequential changes are necessary or desirable in universities' internal procedures. The new arrangements are set out in the UGC's *University Building Projects — Notes on Control and Guidance 1982.*

MINOR WORKS

Prior to 1973/74, the UGC gave each university an annual block allocation for minor building works, such as adaptation of existing accommodation for new uses, improving utilization of existing facilities, and minor extensions to existing buildings. No prior approval was required for starting any single project costing up to £25,000 financed on this basis. From 1973/74 the recurrent grant was increased to include provision for, and a university was free to finance, minor building projects out of general income provided that its total expenditure on all capital items (land, buildings, and associated fees) did not exceed 2½% of recurrent grant. That figure was subsequently cut for that year to 1 7/8% as a means of restraining public expenditure, but since 1977/78 has been 3%. The limit below which projects could be started without specific approval has been increased by stages (and roughly in line with inflation) from £25,000 to the figure of £100,000 referred to above.

Universities are thus faced with two levels of decision, first how far to go towards the 3% limit in setting a budget for minor works, and secondly how to determine which projects are to be financed from the budget. Within the group of universities studied more than half were spending less than 2%. It may or may not be significant that the university with the greatest academic staff involvement in minor works expenditure spends up to the full 3%. It also has a stock of older buildings, however, and its needs therefore may be greater. In some universities it has been the practice to take 3% 'off the top' of the UGC grant for estimating purposes before other budgets are drafted, though the resulting fund is liable to be used later on, or during the financial year, to help cover an overall university deficit. Elsewhere, the minor works budget is 'what can be afforded' and is liable to be hit hard early on. We found only one instance of a multi-year development plan for the university's premises based on minor works. The sum of capital expenditure from revenue for all universities was as high as 2.8% of Exchequer grants in 1977/78 and 2.7% in 1979/80, probably because of grants from the UGC earmarked for health, safety and energy conservation works.

Only one university allows departments to spend any of their allocation from general university funds on minor works, though they may finance minor works from other sources of funds, such as research grants, and from income earning activities, subject of course to central control. Hence the normal practice is for each and every minor alteration proposed for financing from general funds to be considered on a competitive basis by the buildings committee or a sub-committee. There are, however, important differences in approach. Some universities have evolved lists of criteria against which proposals are assessed. The longest comprises ten ranked criteria: eg A, is the job required to comply with statutory requirements? E, would it improve creature comforts? G, could it be deferred for at least 18 months? One university assesses minor works bids according to the following priorities: (a) teaching needs, (b) research needs, (c) health and safety requirements; and gives absolute preference to bids submitted by the academic accommodation committee because this expresses an academic priority. Another university follows what is almost a reverse priority order: (a) health and safety requirements, (b) better security, (c) improvement of obsolescent or substandard facilities, (d) conversion of academic accommodation to correct shortages of departmental space, (e) upgrading of heavily used non-departmental space. Another way a difference of priorities is expressed is in the decision-making process. At one extreme one university takes its decisions through an entirely academic body of Pro-Vice-Chancellors and chairmen of Faculties chaired by the Vice-Chancellor; at the other, the decisions appear to be taken very much by university officers, with the Vice-Chancellor in the chair. At a third university, where expenditure is below 1%, specific sums are allocated to 'academic area' decision-making bodies for their judgement of priorities, with a balance held back for decision by the Vice-Chancellor advised by his senior officers.

A recent report by UGC officers foresaw that universities would need to spend 30% more during the 1980s compared with the late 1970s on adapting and modifying existing buildings if the demands of academic development were to be properly met.

ALLOCATION OF SPACE

For more than a decade up till 1973, when the capital programme was sharply cut for the first time, the allocation of departmental accommodation had not been a serious problem for British universities: the building programme was such that the needs of all departments could be met sooner or later through new construction. Even after 1973 the building programme picked up and accommodation difficulties in non-expanding universities were of a local departmental character rather than institution-wide. Some universities have not, therefore, felt any strong need to integrate the allocation of accommodation with the minor works programme, or either of these with academic planning. But the cessation of new building is forcing all universities to look more closely at departmental use of space, particularly when there appears to be a pressing need for additional space to be allocated to one department which can be met only by withdrawing space from another. In addition, the reduction in overall income, the rising cost of proper maintenance, and the pressure to devote a larger proportion of the budget to academic expenditure, all point to increasing utilization and indeed to reducing the stock of buildings. Although some universities nominally subscribe to a 'zero based' system which implies that all accommodation is in the annual gift of the university, it appears to be the almost universal practice that what a department has it holds and that little if any movement can take place unless the vacating department is offered a substantial carrot in the form of desirable alternative accommodation or some other bonus. If re-allocation of whole departments is difficult there was evidence of at least one university which operated a regular system for annually re-allocating elements of departmental space according to norms for academic staff, research staff and postgraduates, and through a committee of the building committee. This committee also took account of carrell space in the library. It is clear that fluctuations in departmental size, implicit in the UGC's dirigiste policies, and the need to dispose of buildings for reasons of economy or contraction, will require universities to adopt a much firmer policy towards space allocation in the future.

Specific machinery for relating accommodation needs to the minor works building programme and to overall academic planning policy is the exception rather than the rule: only one instance was found of a joint committee of the academic planning committee and the development committee, which made recommendations on bids in the range £8,000 — c.£100,000. It is generally assumed that some overlapping membership or common servicing will ensure all the integration that is required. The overlap may be extensive: at one university the minor works and maintenance committee includes the three Pro-Vice-Chancellors and the four chairmen of Faculty Boards. Some, but not many, universities have amalgamated the accommodation committee and the minor works committees and it would seem inevitable that the reviews being forced upon universities by financial restraints will lead to further examples of greater integration of these activities.

The only significant exception we found to the description above is at Cranfield. There the Estates Officer computes a service cost per square metre which is charged to a department for the space occupied and provides a strong disincentive to hoarding space. Space allocation at the margin is left to market forces.

Now that universities can retain up to £100,000 of the proceeds from each sale of publicly financed premises, there is more incentive generally to release space, though a more powerful incentive might be in retaining income from premises not in normal university use that can be externally let.

MAINTENANCE OF PREMISES; BUILDING SERVICES

This heading embraces the expenses which are incurred in using buildings, and keeping them in use, for their existing purposes. The expenses account for some 17% of universities' recurrent expenditure from total income (nearly 20% from General Income — see Table 3, p. 31). If the occupancy costs that are carried on separate accounts (principally for student accommodation) are estimated and added, the sum of expenditure on all buildings in 1981/82 is probably about £300m and relates to a stock of buildings with a replacement cost of some £7,500m.

The expenses are subdivided on UGC Form 3 between:

	% in 1979/80
Repairs and maintenance	28.0
Cleaning and custodial services	20.4
Heat, light and water	21.7
Telephones	5.4
Rates	19.0
Rent	1.2
Insurance	1.8
Other	2.5
	100.00

The last four items need not be considered specifically: except for local authority rates they are small, and rates are met by a special grant from the UGC so do not have to be provided for in the main university budget.

Repairs and Maintenance
A distinction should be made between routine maintenance and major repairs, the latter being work which should not need to be done more frequently than every ten years (and typically every twenty years), such as replacing central heating systems and asphalt roofs. In the Building Advice Unit report the UGC highlighted the fact that the large stock of buildings constructed in the boom years of 1957 onwards would be between fifteen and twenty-five years old in the 1980s, an age at which maintenance costs rise sharply because major repairs are needed for the first time. The budget requirement for routine maintenance normally appears to be that stated by the Building Officer, based on historical expenditure with an allowance for inflation, new building stock, etc. (The classic means of meeting a shortfall between budget and requirement is of course, to defer interior redecoration.) We found no instance of the requirement being defined by reference to formulae, such as are recommended in textbooks on building maintenance: eg a percentage of the current value or replacement cost of the buildings, or a unit cost per square or cubic metre, except that the latter is used in one university to determine the addition to the budget required in respect of a new building.

Major repairs are variously defined and variously handled. Both a large civic university and a small new university take the view that, one year with another, the cost of exceptional items will average out, and so have a single budget covering both routine maintenance and major repairs.

For the former, having long since entered the cycle of replacements, the assumption may be sound; for the latter, still in the honeymoon with new buildings, an awkward transition to a higher level of expenditure may have to be faced in a few years. Another new university has progressively increased the annual contributions to a major repairs fund so as to ease that transition, though the fund has been raided by the threshold of a major repair being lowered. Another civic university deliberately chose not to create a provision fund because of inflation. One institution runs a modest provision fund for 'catastrophes' in plant breakdown, but not for age and obsolescence.

Cleaning and Custodial Services Cleaning and custodial services are centrally budgeted and managed, except in one university which has devolved the budget to the academic or support unit occupying one or a group of buildings. This university is currently reconsidering its policy in this respect. Only one reference was made to a 'standard' to guide the level of provision, namely that an operative can clean 141m² per hour. Otherwise bids are based on existing commitment plus provision for new buildings, and budget cuts absorbed by vacancies and reorganization of duties.

Heat, Light and Water Again, only one university has devolved to users any part of the expenditure on heat, light and water, by metering electricity in individual buildings. 'Standards' are more in evidence in that lighting and heating levels can be specified by the building committee and controlled by its officers.

Telephones There is widespread interest in controlling the telephone budget by using equipment which monitors each call by extension and by re-charging the full cost to the appropriate department; but only one of the sample institutions has done so. Two others, lacking the equipment, make a flat rate re-charge of line rental and average call charges for each extension. At least two universities have had formulae to determine the level of provision of lines, but ad hoc assessment by the appropriate officer on application from a head of department seems more normal.

ALLOCATION MECHANISMS
A good deal of interest must centre on the mechanism by which funds are allocated under the premises heading. A common method is for the appropriate professional officer(s) to prepare a budget in consultation with the Finance Officer which is then, presumably after approval by the Vice-Chancellor, put to a building or estates committee for final approval by the finance committee. In one university, however, the Registrar himself determines the budget for repairs and maintenance, cleaning, portering, heat, light, water and telephones for submission to the finance committee, and when this budget is finally approved as part of the overall university

budget it is handled by an 'estates group' made up entirely of senior administrators. In another university expenditure on electricity, cleaning, portering and telephones is included in block grants to 'academic areas' and left to them to administer.

It is clear that in many universities planned maintenance schemes or formula-based allocations for say cleaning and portering have broken down under the new 'expenditure led' funding arrangements. The increase in costs of, for example, heat, light, water and power are such that they probably require attack on a broader front than that of a single institution. Our impression is that there are too many universities trying to cope with the problems on a piecemeal basis and that more inter-institutional co-operation could be helpful. In the allocation process budgets for the premises side of university expenditure have not been reduced to the extent that might occur in similar circumstances in industry but even the cuts that have been made have caused considerable dislocation to established practices. Inevitably very few people in universities can work up much interest, except when it affects their area, in policy towards maintenance, repairs, etc. Committees tend to trust their officers and impose equal cuts on all services so that these parts of the budget tend to be scrutinized rather more cursorily than they are on the academic side. This imposes heavy burdens on the professional officers, who are not always in a strong position to propose measures which may be unpopular with their academic colleagues: for example, to 'data log' telephone calls and re-charge them to departments.

NOTES AND REFERENCES
1   UGC *Annual Survey 1965-6* p. 33. HMSO
2   UGC *Annual Survey 1979-80* p. 13. HMSO
3   UGC (1956) *Methods used by Universities of Contracting and of Recording and Controlling Expenditure* (Report of the committee on the control of expenditure from non-recurrent grants, chaired by Sir George Gater) Cmnd 9. HMSO
4   UGC (1960) *Methods used by Universities of Contracting and of Recording and Controlling Expenditure* (Review by Sir Anthony Rucker of the application by universities of the procedures recommended by Sir George Gater's Committee) Cmnd 1235. HMSO
5   UGC (1st edition 1963, 6th edition 1977) *Notes on Procedure: Capital Grants*
6   UGC (1982) *University Building Projects — Notes on Control and Guidance*
7   UGC Building Advice Unit (1980) *University Needs for Maintenance and Minor Works*
8   UGC Building Advice Unit op.cit.

ADMINISTRATION AND CENTRAL SERVICES

This chapter is concerned with that amorphous area of university expenditure covered by Sections 5 and 6 of Table 3 of the UGC Form 3, Administration and Central Services (5) and Staff and Student Facilities and Amenities (6). In addition to staffing costs for the central administration, Section 5 includes a host of subheads such as expenditure on consumables, postage, recruitment expenses, administrative computers, publications (non-educational), etc. Section 6 includes careers advisory services, university health services, accommodation offices, athletic facilities, grants to student societies, the salaries of wardens of halls of residences, deficits on residences and catering, etc.

As in the academic sector we find a diversity of methods of allocation reflecting the history and traditions of institutions as well as the contributions of individuals. Indeed there are many examples where individual officers have left a clear mark of their own personality, judgement and occasionally prejudice on the policies of the institution or in the composition of the details of the heads of expenditure to be submitted to the appropriate authority.

The diversity of method, the paucity of hard information and the acquired caution of administrators make it very difficult to quantify and assess the results of any examination of the processes of allocation on an inter-university basis: description is easy enough, though even here, establishing a clear chain of allocation procedures with the crucial decision points evident is not always straightforward. It would be pointless to seek to suggest that all allocation processes conform to some basic model. They patently do not, for they start from different concepts of the process involved. For some the start is what is needed to do the job ahead — the aggregation of a number of claims, each modified at certain more or less understood points in the chain, into a total bid against available resources. For others the process is quite the reverse: a determination of the cost of the existing activities set against expected total funds available and informed advice on the general division of 'free monies' for agreed purposes (eg academic sector, non-academic sector including administration and certain central services and the students union) followed by a more detailed and argued distribution of the funds available.

Not only is it clear that the procedures for allocation have different conceptual bases, but the administrative framework which each institution has devised imposes its own obligations. Size itself dictates in some measure the approach and the level of detail at which the claim is finally judged. The complexity of a university's governing processes adds another, so that the stages through which a claim needs to go before it emerges as an allocation differ widely. Furthermore, the prevailing attitude to the management of a university's resources is influential. The evidence suggests that those universities where the general administration, the stewardship of finance and the management of the estate are separate domains tend to arrange their processes of resource allocation, and in particular their committee structures, differently from those universities where virtually the whole of the non-academic sector is administered and managed by one senior officer, although in this latter group it is by no means the case that the senior officer presents each claim on his personal authority to each decision point in the structure. In investigating the procedures used by the universities in the survey it became clear that it would be more fruitful to try to describe those central features which were clear and had some air of permanence in order to highlight points of importance and to seek to draw out some of the points on which there is less clarity and which therefore deserve some discussion.

The general picture is that in almost all universities the previous year's experience is the dominant factor in formulating the estimates of expenditure for administration and central services. As one would expect, attempts are made to anticipate any significant change in circumstances and costs. Formulae are not used and much depends on the experience, intuition and detailed researches of senior administrative officers. In most cases senior officers in close consultation with the Finance Officer are the major formulators of policy. It is natural to assume that the Vice-Chancellor will play a significant, if not official role in establishing the assumptions and attitudes which receive expression in the detailed compilation of the claims for increased resources. Additionally, the way in which the claims of services such as the careers advisory services or the accommodation office are drawn up may well be influenced by the assessment made by the officer(s) responsible of the prevailing attitude in the university amongst significant groups or individuals to the need for and role of those services.

In one university it was clear that if monies were available after existing commitments had been met the academic sector had an automatic allocation based on agreed norms in relation to increased student numbers. Any residue was then distributed to academic services and the non-academic activities. How common an approach to the distribution of free monies this represents is not clear. While the approach has a distinct appeal since it represents a practical expression of the primacy of academic needs, it does depend for its effectiveness on a general consensus that the norms, etc. are themselves reasonable and provide some re-assurance that the claims of the academic sector will not run away with the whole process of resource allocation.

Table 18 summarizes the committees responsible for the allocation of resources for administration and central services and the officers whose duty it is to provide the groundwork for those committees. (Note: This is a picture of the situation in 1979/80.) The Council (Court in Scotland) of each institution, either itself or on the recommendation of a finance committee, remains in all universities the final arbiter of the sums made available to administrative and central services areas. Given the Council's final responsibility for the good management of the university, it is of course not surprising that the authority to approve the overall budgetary dispositions has been retained by the body which is ultimately responsible. Nevertheless there is still an area of uncertainty in how real the final authority is, since many of the answers revealed that increases in expenditure were written into budgets on the basis of officers' judgements and were not always made explicit in the submission to the appropriate committee. For example, there are at least three causes of increased recruitment advertising costs: inflation, increased turnover/new posts, increased coverage (either in frequency of advertisement or in the spread of newspapers in which the advertisement is placed). Inflation increases are normally spelled out in a general way in the presentation of a budget. Expected new posts and significant increases in turnover will usually be noted, but it is very doubtful if there is any discussion of the cost and extent of advertising for any particular kind of posts. The example given is minor, but the underlying argument extends to all items of administrative expense. It is, of course, possible to argue that it is not practicable to control some of these costs or that the result of refining the budget presentation is not worth the effort. That, however, is not a question for administrators to answer but for the appropriate authority within the resource allocation structure. (Furthermore, the appropriate authority should not automatically be defined as an additional special committee.) One of the most difficult questions for a university to answer is 'To whom and to what extent should discretionary powers be given?' The point of principle under discussion here is not whether university administrators should exercise judgement, but whether they should exercise it in such a way as to pre-empt other decisions about the disposition of financial and other resources. The answer must be that they, no more than academics, should pre-empt resources by the exercise of discretionary powers, or in the exercise of their professional responsibilities.

What is important is that the assumptions which find their way into the preparation of the budget should be made explicit and these assumptions should be tested regularly at an appropriate point in the allocation process. This is, of course, a general requirement with relevance in all areas of the university's expenditure. But it is questionable whether the type of questions asked and of judgement exercised in scrutinizing, for example, the academic budget, are applied in the same rigorous way in the assessment of the needs of the administration and central services. The process of drawing up the budget and of making allocations obviously involves judgements; and decisions such as whether x or y should have a secretary, or a or b should have additional administrative assistance are continually being made. What is not so clear, however, is whether the process facilitates or can even allow for questioning of the policies and assumptions underlying particular claims in cases where perhaps a reorganization of the overall deployment of resources, rather than adjustments within particular budget heads, would more effectively achieve the desired end.

The basis of the actual arguments put forward is clear, however, from the descriptions of the procedures involved in individual universities. In one university consumable expenditure by the administration is relatively low and is determined annually upon need, and provided it is kept to a reasonable level compared with the previous period, and is in line with general university policies, it would automatically be built into the annual and revised estimates. In the same university, publications and general advertising are treated in the same way as consumable expenditure. In another, estimates for these heads are calculated largely on the basis of historic costs, taking account of any anticipated changes in the volume of activity in the ensuing year. In a third university an assessment is made of trends of the previous year's expenditure to determine the new base, to which is added the full year's effect of inflation plus or minus anticipated variations. In yet another university, the comment is offered that the Finance Officer estimates needs on the basis of his experience without reference to other officers.

There is, interestingly, a great variation in the detail in which figures are presented to the appropriate committee. Some committees are provided with budgets which detail expenditures of £100 on individual items, while others deal more with the general policies of expenditure and do not appear to find it sensible to discuss the minute details of activities of which they have only a superficial knowledge. While this is a natural development of each university's growth, it serves only to cloud any overall assessment of the underlying principles on which resources are allocated to central administration and to central services. The task is further complicated by the separation in some universities between decisions on staffing and decisions on other expenditures. It is not clear that this particular separation improves the quality of the decisions made or makes the process or judgement any more logical.

No doubt the influence of Vice-Chancellors, Treasurers, Registrars and Secretaries, Finance Officers and other senior members of the non-academic staff has in each university been considerable in determining the degree of detail with which the information is presented to the allocating body. It is nonetheless noteworthy that within the group of universities studied none has enunciated clearly its assessment of the priorities of presentation and discussion and decision which underlie the allocation of resources to the central administration and central services. Again, the point which is at issue is that there is almost no evidence from a representative sample of institutions which suggests that university officers responsible for the services under examination have the will, the appropriate management information, or indeed the time to re-assess regularly, systematically, and in concert with those most affected by their activities, the priorities and practices of that unit for which each of them is responsible. No doubt many universities will point to advisory or even management committees for services such as the careers service or the accommodation office; and to a greater or lesser extent they fulfil part of the role suggested above. It is not clear, however, that such separate committees are either necessary or the most useful way of exercising an effective management role. By their nature they will more appropriately exercise an advisory function. Indeed they may in some cases (eg committees with responsibilities for university crèches, counselling services, etc.) act as a pressure group and be seen by the head of the service concerned to be natural allies in the fight for a greater share of the available resources. In all likelihood they will not be encouraged to make the critical managerial assessments needed to place the claims of a particular service in the context of the needs of a group of similar services or of the university as a whole.

The positions of responsibility and trust accorded to senior administrative officers in both the general and the particular resource allocation process are undeniable. One obvious difference is that between the multi-headed structure and the unitary. Essentially, in the multi-headed structure, the formal position is that each senior officer makes his case to the appropriate committee and his claim is judged in the context of others. In the unitary structure there are examples where the Registrar/Secretary presents a single case in which he, fulfilling the Fielden and Lockwood role of a central co-ordinator [1], in concert with his colleagues and in consultation with his Vice-Chancellor, has already made judgements about priorities, since in the nature of things it would not be usual for him to present — any more than an academic head of department will present — a list of 'failed claims' to the allocating committee. There are also examples where the single chief officer does not involve himself regularly in the creation and presentation of certain of the claims for resources. One important influence in this respect is almost certainly the size of the university and the complexity of its committee procedures. A continuing dilemma for the university is the natural tension between 'real work' and overheads: that is to say between expenditure on academic departments and services and all other expenditure. The influence of academics on the resolution of this dilemma and in particular on the allocation of resources to administration and central services, varies considerably from the broad brush division of resources to the major areas of the university (with a monitoring through the report of individual decisions thereafter) to involvement in the detail of the determination of quite discrete items of expenditure, for example through a Senate committee which makes no provision for lay influence (see Table 19 for the way in which administrative staffing claims are dealt with) or through an academic-dominated sub-committee of the finance committee of Council.

The most frequently cited justification for the growth in administrative staff up to 1980 is need, although it is not always the central administrators themselves who have always promoted such claims. The creation of posts for schools liaison officers, public relations officers, safety officers, student counsellors, university physicians, etc., often originated as much in the judgements and initiatives of academic or lay members of the institutions as in the aspirations of senior administrators.

Information on the numbers of administrative staff in the universities under consideration is given in Table 20. In Fielden and Lockwood there is a proposal for the number of administrative staff needed for a university of 5,000-7,000 students using the suggested administrative structure. The figures proposed are a range of 50-70, some 30% of whom would be in senior positions. The authors deny that they are using a norm of one administrative member of staff (on academic-related pay scales) to every hundred students.[2] The evidence in Table 20 suggests that they would have been wrong to do so; it also suggests that it might be possible to expect significant economies of scale, although Pickford argues that above 4,000 students economies of scale are marginal.[3] Fielden and Lockwood avoid discussion of their illustrative judgements by refraining from making their reasoning explicit, on the grounds that what they have done is to give illustrations, not prescriptions. It seems clear that we have not advanced beyond the stage Fielden and Lockwood explored a decade ago, nor have we advanced beyond the belief that illustrative comparisons between universities are useful for others but do not apply to ourselves. There is no suggestion that even rough and ready guidelines, for example the ratio of administrative to academic staff posts, are used in any of the universities in the survey.

The separation between academic and other expenditure is in one sense unreal. There is, however, a natural concern that the sheer size of the academic claim will override the necessary provisions for other sectors. It is, for example, clear that for a variety of reasons the externally generated administrative load of universities has increased, but it is not so immediately ascertainable* as an increased teaching load or increased research expenditure, while the development of more refined and in some ways sophisticated governmental processes within the institution has carried with it a corresponding pressure on both academic and administrative time. The resource allocation process should ideally, therefore, provide for a judicious blend of academic and lay influence to determine the allocation of resources to administration, if only because those systems which ignore

---

*At the time of the first legislation on industrial relations and employment contracts, one university professor when the Senate was advised of some of the implications was heard to say 'But this (legislation) surely isn't meant to apply to universities.'

the lay influence or the academic influence can ultimately be abused or resented in a period of stress, with unhappy consequences for the health of the total system.

The requirement of the central administration for resources depends upon a series of tasks which in general terms is the same in every university: eg servicing committees, keeping records, paying bills, admitting students etc. What is not common to every university is the expectation each one has of each of its services or its organization of them, with the result that at one level it is possible to demonstrate that every university is unique and that no worthwhile comparisons are possible. Work has been done on the expenditure of universities on administration which seeks to make some statistical comparisons but Pickford concludes that 'it is difficult to believe that the administrations of such universities as X are providing the same level of service as those of Y.'[4] This suggests, therefore, that while a series of comparisons, for example those in **Tables 19** and **21**, should be useful as a general background to considering the resource needs of the administration, those responsible for resource allocation must also look to a series of internal assessments to assist them in judging the needs of a central service like the careers service, the accommodation service or the central administration.[5] Careers services share on a confidential basis the kind of information which would be a most useful background to the consideration of their staffing and other resource levels but it is released to member services in such a way as to preserve the anonymity of institutions.

All the indications in the data collected show that administrative and other central staff in a university are generally considered to be efficient (by nature and by training), cost conscious, and aware that their role is to use effectively and efficiently the resources made available to them to support the academic and other essential activities of their institutions. However, there is little to indicate that universities have developed those systems of monitoring of expenditures (including the time of staff) which will provide the evidence on which judgements of priorities and needs can be undertaken.[6]

In reply to a question about monitoring effectiveness the following kinds of response illustrate the general acceptance of the principle of monitoring for value for money but the failure or perhaps the real difficulties of giving it practical expression.

'No, in any strict sense — there is no management services officer. The chief administratative officers are responsible for the effective deployment of administrative time and effort, i.e. they fight amongst themselves as to which posts should be filled or frozen.'

'Except for ad hoc reviews and review when new appointments or promotions are being proposed there is no regular monitoring and evaluation of the (effective) deployment of administrative staff.'

'Monitoring and evaluating the effective deployment of administrative time and effort is a function carried out as part of the day-to-day activities of senior managements.'

While there is little evidence of a move by universities towards 'value for money' reviews, other enterprises are beginning to explore the possibility. For example, within the Health Service, there has been a recent marked move towards accountability for the use of time and resources. There are reports that formal reporting is being introduced on a trial basis in some area health authorities, with an agreed review system, embracing norms for the standards of care, levels of staffing, etc., against which actual performance can be judged. Leading industrial concerns (eg Shell and ICI) incorporate, in part, the idea of effectiveness reviews in personnel evaluation procedures in which they call for assessments of the performance of staff, of how time was spent, and of the effectiveness of the individual. A central feature of such systems is that the manager and the managed are required to address themselves to these questions rigorously and yet sympathetically. The Civil Service carries out methodical reviews of its staff, many of whom are engaged in work no more directed to measurable output than is the work of university administrators and others in the central services.

The administration and central services area accounts on average for no more than 6% of a university's expenditure. Savings, therefore, through efficiency and strict budgetary control offer less return for effort than savings elsewhere in the system. Given, however, the absolute expenditures involved, an outside observer would expect to find some widespread evidence of the regular critical and systematic review of efficiency and effectiveness. There is from the universities surveyed evidence of no more than managerial nods in this direction. Ad hoc surveys and investigations of administrative practices and requirements have been undertaken on a wide front by O & M units in universities. It would be useful to know if one of the suggestions is for periodic and systematic review of the functions undertaken and the resources needed for their discharge.

Perhaps the difficult financial situation universities now face will prompt a more explicit and articulated 'value for money' approach to the control of staff, time and cash: 'less what do we need to do the job but how do we best use the limited resources available to us.' Indicative of the trend in this direction is evidence that cash allocations for administrative purposes are seen less as broad indicators of likely spending than as hard cash-limited budgets, with named individuals made responsible for the management of the cash as part of their normal duties. It is clear that this trend will and must develop not only as a positive response to the problems of cash-limited allocations but as a method of obtaining some reliable information for use in judging what resources should be and can be made available to administration and central services.

There is no evidence for the use of internal but unpublished yardsticks

TABLE 18
Committees and officers responsible for consideration and approval of resource allocation for administration and central services 1979/80

University	Specialist committee	General finance committee	Level of detail at effective decision level	Officers (in addition to Registrar/Secretary)
A	Special group of Council for establishment of staff	Finance and general purposes committee	Significant oversight of expenditure for whole budget	Principal Administrative Officer
B	Resources committee	Finance board	Significant detail for resources committee and more broadly for finance board	Finance Officer
C	Sub-committee for staffing proposals	Finance committee	Significant detail for staffing. More broad consideration for other items	Accountant
D	Budget sub-committee	Finance committee	Considerable detail	Finance Officer
E	Committee of colleges Building committee	Finance committee	Considerable detail for finance committee	Finance Officer (in consultation with senior officers)

F	Specialist committee for staff and finance executive sub-committee	Finance committee	Considerable detail for sub-committee	Bursar
G	Sub-committee for approval of detail of additional staffing	Finance committee	Global for new resources (if required): detailed for existing commitment	Deputy Registrar (finance)
H	Specialist sub-committee in various areas including a Committee of Deans for new posts	Finance committee	Detailed consideration for each broad grouping	Director of Finance
I	Specialist staff committee and resources sub-committee of finance committee	General purposes committee	Considerable detail	Finance Officer
J	Specialist staff sub-committee of finance committee	Finance and general purposes committee	Considerable detail for sub-committee	Academic Registrar Finance Officer

TABLE 19
Comparison of the numbers of administrative staff in ten universities

University	Academic staff 31.12.79 *	Student nos. FTE 31.12.79 *	Total expend. 1979/80 £000 *	Admin. expend. 1979/80 £000 +	% expend. on admin.	Admin. staff 31.12.79 ++	Academic staff per admin. staff member	Students per admin. staff member
A	374	3,788	12,328	765	6.2	60	6.2	63
B	379	4,118	13,131	963	7.3	33	11.5	125
C	1,183	10,010	46,831	2,411	5.2	75.5	15.7	133
D	268	2,977	9,272	790	8.5	23	11.7	129
E	483	4,732	13,484	745	5.5	46	10.5	103
F	1,082	10,829	40,591	2,403	5.9	87	12.4	124
G	491	4,958	16,907	1,304	7.7	48	10.2	103
H	897	7,995	30,114	1,809	6.0	104	8.6	77
I	453	4,378	16,218	1,221	7.5	66	6.9	66
J	503	5,106	16,820	1,168	6.9	45	11.2	113
	6,113	58,891	215,696	13,579	6.3	587.5	10.4	100

* Information obtained from *Statistics of Education* Vol. 6
+ UGC Form 3
+ + In USR Present Employment Codes 31, 32, 33, 34, 35, 36, 37 (Manual of Operating Procedure revised and re-issued March 1976, p. 21)

TABLE 20
Machinery for considering claims for administrative staff posts 1979/80

University	Machinery
A	Special panel of Council
B	Sub-committee of resources committee for all budget (staffing and non-staffing) costs
C	Administrative staff appointments committee reporting to the staff committee
D	General budget committee; specialist budgets vetted by Registrar and Finance Officer before presentation
E	New posts and gradings tightly controlled
	i for all non-USS posts via a Pro-Vice-Chancellor;
	ii for USS posts by the developments committee reporting to Senate after consultation with any appropriate specialist committee, then to finance committee for recommendation to Council
F	Planning committee of Senate
G	Council committee if part of global resource available to non-academic area is to be used for staff
H	All new posts to be approved by specialist sub-committee reporting to Committee of Deans
I	Planning committee
J	Specialist committee

for the numbers and kinds of administrators. Nor is there evidence that in the process of judging the resources necessary for a university administration there is the systematic use of external evidence of any kind. There are, in this area too, practical difficulties in collecting, tabulating and comparing evidence and in knowing that variations occur in the treatment of items of expenditure by Finance Officers in compiling UGC returns and university accounts. Table 21, therefore, sets out some key inter-institutional indications[7] which institutions and committees may find useful as an aid to decision-making in regard to resource allocation to administration and central services.

TABLE 21
Key inter-institutional comparators for resource allocation to administration
and central services

The purpose of inter-university comparison is to bring out wide variations
from the norm and to enable such variations to be examined and justified
by the particular circumstances, policies or practices of the institution
concerned.

The following data relate to one institution in a group of 23 and are
used with that university's permission.

The figures derive from provisional Form 3 1980-81 data (E & OE) and
have been supplied by courtesy of USR and worked out by its Executive
Secretary Dr A.W. Nichol.

			£000
1	Total expenditure	Highest	25,654
		Lowest	10,768
		Median	15,844
		Total	364,521
		Mean Value	15,849 nearest university
			is number 12 with £15,844
		University x is number 2 with £21,470	

			£000
2	Expenditure on	Highest	4,095
	research grants and	Lowest	608
	contracts	Median	1,395
		Total	37,517
		Mean Value	1,631 nearest university
			is number 10 with £1,627
		University x is number 15 with £1,137	

			%
3	Percentage on research	Highest	20.247
	grants and contracts	Lowest	5.296
		Median	8.986
		Mean Value	9.99 nearest university
			is number 11 with 9.87%
		University x is number 23 with 5.296%	

continued

TABLE 21 continued

			£000
4	Academic staff wholly supported by UGC	Highest	483
		Lowest	260
		Median	382
		Total	8,527
		Mean Value	371 nearest university is number 13 with 372

University x is number 3 with 478

			£000
5	All academic staff	Highest	660
		Lowest	302
		Median	453
		Total	10,542
		Mean Value	458 nearest university is number 11 with 461

University x is number 7 with 508

			%
6	Percentage UGC funded	Highest	94.094
		Lowest	69.242
		Median	81.263
		Mean Value	81.40 nearest university is number 12 with 81.26%

University x is number 1 with 94.094%

			%
7	Total 'student load' (Form 3) divided by total academic staff	Highest	9.921
		Lowest	6.004
		Median	8.231
		Mean Value	8.17 nearest university is number 13 with 8.16

University x is number 2 with 9.480

			£000
8	Administration expenditure (Form 3 Col 45)	Highest	1,651
		Lowest	609
		Median	983
		Total	23,498
		Mean Value	1,022 nearest university is number 9 with £1,012

University x is number 3 with £1,391

continued

TABLE 21 continued

			%
9	Administration expenditure as a percentage of the total	Highest	8.223
		Lowest	5.050
		Median	6.425
		Mean Value	6.50 nearest university is number 10 with 6.48%

University x is number 10 with 6.479%

			£000
10	Administration expenditure divided by student load (£000 per student)	Highest	0.389
		Lowest	0.189
		Median	0.289
		Mean Value	0.28 nearest university is number 13 with £0.27

University x is number 12 with £0.289

			£000
11	Premises expenditure (Form 3 Col 42)	Highest	4,529
		Lowest	1,258
		Median	2,580
		Total	61,263
		Mean Value	2,664 nearest university is number 11 with £2,698

University x is number 2 with £3,795

			%
12	Premises expenditure as a percentage of total expenditure	Highest	22.623
		Lowest	11.109
		Median	17.391
		Mean Value	16.88 nearest university is number 13 with 16.58%

University x is number 10 with 17.676%

			£
13	Premises expenditure per FTE Student	Highest	1.150
		Lowest	0.424
		Median	0.699
		Mean Value	0.73 nearest university is number 11 with £0.73

University x is number 8 with £0.788

continued

TABLE 21 continued

			£000
14	Library expenditure	Highest	1,136
	(Form 3 Col 11)	Lowest	336
		Median	655
		Total	15,964
		Mean Value	694 nearest university is number 10 with £713

University x is number 8 with £744

			%
15	Library expenditure	Highest	5.861
	as a percentage of	Lowest	1.633
	total expenditure	Median	4.805
		Mean Value	4.49 nearest university is number 15 with 4.34%

University x is number 20 with 3.465%

			£000
16	Expenditure on other	Highest	982
	academic services	Lowest	290
	(museums, computers,	Median	566
	education technology,	Total	12,998
	miscellaneous) (Form 3	Mean Value	565 nearest university is number 12 with £566
	Cols 12-24)		

University x is number 4 with £753

			£
17	Other academic	Highest	0.296
	services: expenditure	Lowest	0.081
	per student	Median	0.145
		Mean Value	0.16 nearest university is number 11 with £0.15

University x is number 10 with £0.156

			%
18	Research income as a	Highest	20.120
	percentage of total	Lowest	5.296
	income	Median	8.705
		Mean Value	9.83 nearest university is number 11 with 9.68%

University x is number 23 with 5.296%

continued

TABLE 21 continued

			%
19	UGC income as a	Highest	94.238
	percentage of total	Lowest	55.825
	income	Median	65.880
		Mean Value	65.87 nearest university is number 12 with 65.88%

University x is number 3 with 70.014%

			%
20	Percentage of post-	Highest	24.888
	graduate students	Lowest	7.418
		Median	17.150
		Mean Value	16.30 nearest university is number 13 with 16.33%

University x is number 19 with 12.811%

21	Administrative staff	Highest	55
	wholly supported by	Lowest	19
	UGC	Median	32
		Mean Value	33 nearest university is number 11 with 33

University x is number 6 with 42

22	All administrative staff	Highest	56
		Lowest	19
		Median	33
		Mean Value	33 nearest university is number 12 with 33

University x is number 6 with 42

23	Academic staff per	Highest	21.48
	staff member (Form 3	Lowest	9.81
	Cols 22)	Median	13.38
		Mean Value	14.58 nearest university is number 10 with 14.39

University x is number 17 with 12.10

continued

TABLE 21 continued

24	Students per administrative staff member (Form 3 Cols 22)	Highest	185.1
		Lowest	83.8
		Median	124.6
		Mean Value	125.5 nearest university is number 12 with 124.6

University x is number 15 with 119.0

25	Administration expenditure per student		£
		Highest	361
		Lowest	178
		Median	258
		Mean Value	260 nearest university is number 11 with £260

University x is number 10 with £278

26	Administration expenditure per staff member (Form 3 Col 4)		£
		Highest	3,762
		Lowest	1,704
		Median	2,805
		Mean Value	2,790 nearest university is number 13 with £2,790

University x is number 10 with £2,910

27	Administration expenditure per staff member (Form 3 Col 5)		£
		Highest	2,815
		Lowest	1,466
		Median	2,313
		Mean Value	2,260 nearest university is number 13 with £2,790

University x is number 2 with £2,738

NOTES AND REFERENCES
1 Fielden, J. and Lockwood, G. (1973) *Planning and Management in Universities* p. 93. Chatto and Windus/Sussex University Press
2 Fielden, J. and Lockwood, G. op.cit. p. 188
3 Pickford, M. (1974) A Statistical analysis of university administrative expenditure *Iournal of the Royal Statistical Society* A. 137 (1) 35
4 Pickford, M. op.cit. p. 44
5 Fielden and Lockwood (op.cit. p. 193) made essentially the same points in their comments on the cost of central administrations and the levels of service required.
6 Fielden and Lockwood (op.cit. p. 264) argued for the introduction of such procedures across the whole of the university
7 Fielden and Lockwood (op.cit. p. 212) see norms as ways of avoiding arguments without guaranteeing a *correct* allocation of resources.

RESOURCE ALLOCATION IN US UNIVERSITIES

Strict comparisons between UK and US higher education are not, of course, possible because of the greater size and diversity of the US system. US higher education is decentralized and constitutionally, as well as practically, a state not a federal responsibility, although federal agencies play a significant role in funding particular research and student aid programmes. On average, prior to the first Reagan budget, state universities received around 44% of their income from their states and around 15% from the Federal Government.[1] By comparison British universities received about 88% from DES sources — UGC, research councils and home fees which are DES controlled (see Table 1, p. 25). Of the 3,000 or so institutions in the United States a significant number are funded privately rather than from state or other public sources and private institutions account for about 25% of the total student population. Higher education covers a more diversified range of institutions than in Britain and includes two-year colleges, community colleges and some state colleges which in Britain correspond more closely to further education than to higher education.

At the state level higher education is controlled or co-ordinated by a number of mechanisms, the most common being a state co-ordinating commission. Some states adopt an alternative system, merging their various institutions into one legal structure governed by a single Board of Regents. Thus in Indiana, for example, a higher education commission acts as a kind of UGC buffer between the Governor's office and the state legislature and the universities, while in Wisconsin the University of Wisconsin covers all universities and colleges in the state and its President and his staff not only run the University of Wisconsin system under the university's Board of Regents but also represent the crucial interface with the state's budget office and legislative apparatus. But the remit of state commissions and other central bodies varies enormously: sometimes they represent a politically neutered body which carries out a more or less passive function while the real bargaining goes on between the individual institutions and the Governor's budget officers; sometimes they cover private as well as public institutions; sometimes they are advisory and sometimes they have statutory powers. The mechanisms and politics of resource allocation to higher education can thus vary considerably from state to state.

In the period of university expansion post-1960 there was an increasing tendency for states to move over to some system of formula budgeting. According to Dr Gross, twenty-two states in 1979 were fully committed to this approach.[2] In practice, almost all states use formulae for some part of the budget and enrolment figures are an important determinant in every state. The following advantages are said to accrue from the formula approach:

a The lessening of political warfare among, and open lobbying by, state-supported institutions for scarce funds.
b The assurance of annual operating appropriations for institutions based on quantifiable objective measures.
c The provision to state officials of a reasonably simple and under- standable basis for deciding upon the appropriation requests of individual institutions.
d The representation of a reasonable compromise between state control over line-item budgeting and institutional fiscal autonomy.[3]

The formula budget represents the form in which a budget request is submitted, not the actual funds allocated. Such budgets will generally use different formulae for different areas of institutional activity: instruction, academic support (including libraries), organized research, public service, student services, physical plant operation and maintenance, and institutional administration. (The comparable UGC expenditure headings are as follows: academic, academic services, general educational, administration, premises, staff and student amenities and miscellaneous.) Each of these areas is defined by workload measures, enrolments, credit hours, unit costs on FTE posts, square footage of building and grounds, and so forth. They invariably represent the result of lengthy bargaining and compromises between state and university officials. Basically there are two formula budgeting methods: at average costs and at marginal costs. Under the first method students are costed at an average, so that when enrolments rise or fall the funding requirement follows suit. Under marginal costing an institution gains much less by increases and loses more slowly in a period of decline.

The problem with formulae, however, as we have found in formula budgeting approaches within universities in Britain (see Chapter 6), is that they are not sufficiently flexible. Most budget formulas are zero based so that a decline in enrolments or a change in the composition of the student body can produce alarming fluctuations in income. Moreover, they are rarely able to discriminate successfully between institutions and recognize quality. It is interesting that a recent study found that of forty-three US universities which had top ranked faculties or departments only six were state universities subject to formula budgeting and these six had only nineteen, or 9.3%, of the top ranked departments. And of these the University of Wisconsin - Madison accounted for twelve. By contrast eighteen state universities in non-formula states accounted for 35.1% of the top ranked departments and the remaining 55.6% were located in nineteen private universities.[4] But the further problem with formula budgeting is that it needs a commitment, which many states have been unable to give, that funds will be available to match the product of the formula.

In the US state university system the internal resource allocation exercise is carried out in two parts: the first through the budget request cycle and the second when the budget is finally approved. The first is an exceptionally long drawn out process, the second may take no more than a few days. In this it contrasts with the British system where, since the breakdown of the quinquennial planning cycle, the formulation of the bid to the UGC is generally regarded as a fairly technical exercise, but the allocation process, when the grant is eventually received, is the subject of lengthy consideration, much heartache, and a great deal of committee activity. There is considerable variety among universities in their approaches to drawing up the budget. In the past they were categorized as 'every tub on its own bottom', or 'the king's decree', or 'the squeaky wheel gets the grease', while nowadays, 'the formula budget', 'the incremental budget', 'PPBS' or 'zero-based budgeting', have taken over as descriptions of different methods. In practice the formula budget and the incremental budget are the most commonly used. In the state universities budgeting is often undertaken on a two-year cycle.[5] This begins with the university administration laying down budget protocols, a set of basic constraints, priorities and planning assumptions to which the operational budgetary units then respond. Academic departments submit their budget requests to the Dean, who in turn submits a consolidated budget request for his college or school to the academic Vice-President. The managerial side of the university will submit its requests through the appropriate hierarchy to a Vice-President for business and finance. The overall budget request, academic and managerial, will be settled by the President and ultimately the Board of Regents. The Board of Regents is a lay body which in effect delegates to the President its powers to run the institution, but as the body legally charged with the management of the institution it must approve the overall budget. At each level the delegation of executive decision-making to university officers like Vice-Presidents, Deans and so forth, rather than to committees makes for an important difference from the British style of university management. In US higher education, authority and decision-making is lodged in individual positions not committees. In particular is this true for decisions about hiring and firing, and about major matters of university policy. Committees, however, do play a significant part in the process. The American Association of University Professors (AAUP) has adopted a formal policy on academic participation in the institutional budget through a representative committee[6] and it is usual in the leading universities for a budgetary committee advisory to the President to play a significant role in the budgetary process. In the University of California, for example, the Senate budget committee meets monthly and its chairman sits on the President's budget committee. Indeed, in some universities, such committees may even play a dominant role.

It might be thought that private universities would order themselves differently but in fact, certainly as regards the major research-based institutions, the process is very similar to the public universities up to this point, though the cycle is usually annual rather than biennial. At Stanford a budget protocol, a document of a dozen or so pages, is issued in October summarizing the financial projections for the budget period and outlining the principal issues and questions pertaining to each budgetary unit. In 1981/82 for example it drew attention to the fact that 'our unrestricted income will in all probability not increase at the same rate as our expenses... [and that] the President and Provost are not in a position to 'hold harmless' any unit against the fact of rising costs.'[7] The Deans then reviewed their academic area in consultation with the departments with a view to economizing on, or cutting out, existing functions and listing new programmes or costs in a priority order. In the meantime the university advisory committee on budget planning reviews the assumptions on which the operating budget planning is based and advises the President. The Operating Budget Guidelines 1981/82 describes the system as follows:

'The principal objective of Stanford's budgeting is to come as close as possible in the allotted time to consensus about general and specific needs, opportunities and constraints. This is in many areas accomplished through a dialectical process in which financial conditions and academic service goals take turns serving as a context for one another. When conditions are the context for goals, the goals are designed, examined and re-designed to become congruent with the University's short and longer term financial possibilities. When the goals are the context for the conditions, the conditions are examined, challenged, re-conceptualized and tested to assure that they are as ample and appropriate as they can be made to be.'[8]

It is clear that the budget process at Stanford is the key resource allocation instrument which determines 'difficult choices among major alternatives.'[9]

Of course at Stanford, once the budget process is complete, and providing there is no sharp change in the university's financial fortunes, the allocations are effectively made for the next year. In the public university system, however, the budget then moves up to the state budget review level where it is then taken up by the co-ordinating commission or post-secondary education agencies, the staff of the governor's executive budget office and the staff attached to the legislature. The power and influence of the Governor's budget office and the legislative staff budget office have grown very considerably in recent years, so that co-ordinating commission reviews may sometimes be rendered nugatory. Indeed there is a surfeit of budget reviews going on often simultaneously, as parts of the budget are proceeding through the appropriations committee of the legislature. In practice higher education appropriations tend to be decided only late in the year because many other items in the state budget are non-discretionary. Thus the basis for the funding of some state services is written into the state's statutes, while appropriations for welfare, transportation and highways are governed by requirements to match federal grants. The result is that higher education is settled towards the end of the legislative session in part on the basis of the resources available after other commitments have been met.

As a consequence, when resources eventually find their way to the institutions, the actual allocations must be carried out at great speed. In principle, because of the commitment to the budget process, funds are normally distributed in line with the original request, although in practice universities have sometimes incurred considerable unpopularity both within and outside the institution by re-directing funds towards favoured projects or schools. Where, however, the budget is reduced or legislative directives are attached to the appropriations bill then a re-allocation must take place. Cuts and legislative directions, which are often instructions passed down from the Governor's office, are on the increase as higher education moves into a steady state or enrolment decline and as fiscal pressures on state governments increase. Inevitably these necessary re-allocations must be accomplished quickly and are carried out by the President and his senior staff, sometimes in conjunction with the advisory budget committees referred to above.

To British eyes it is particularly instructive to examine how the US system has adjusted to the problem of resource allocation in a period of uncertainty which has combined financial restraint and contraction in enrolments. It is difficult to make generalized comparisons with the situation in Britain but it is apparent that the severe economies which first affected British universities in 1973/74 were also experienced, with varying degrees of intensity, across the states and have persisted since. Enrolments have peaked and indeed fallen in some states, or within some parts of states, as the high participation rate has levelled out and begun to fall. The future prospect of longer-term demographic falls in student numbers, enhanced in some parts of the country by population movements to the Sunbelt states, offers a scenario of future instability for higher education as a whole, though not necessarily for the major private universities where the demand for places is expected to remain high. Thus the US system entered a period of instability at about the same time as Britain in 1973-4-5 but unlike Britain it appears to have learned to adapt its procedures to the new environment. In particular, US universities have learned to live with a much more bumpy and uncertain economic climate. The fact that higher education appropriations are settled only late in the legislative session leaves university budgets vulnerable to the effects of sudden federal cutbacks in other state services, so that higher education has to compete over a short time-scale with unexpected demands on the state budget. The effect of Proposition 13 or equivalent tax cutting moves in a number of states was, for example, suddenly to remove the property tax base which gave security to higher education budgets. The growing popular discontent with the image of higher education has also played a significant part in the demands by conservative political groups within the legislature for budget reductions. The cost and bureaucratic inconvenience of federally imposed legislation, such as affirmative action programmes, which are not included in state appropriations, have added irrecoverable financial burdens and political wear and tear on to already hard-pressed university administrations.[10]

The reaction in US higher education to this situation has been energetic and resourceful. At the political level universities, and particularly the public universities, have a long tradition of fighting their corner against the Governor, the legislature, and their respective staffs. They are naturally more populist than their British equivalents and they recognize, in a way that their British counterparts seem not to do, that universities must be justified to the outside world. The US reaction to the 1981 cuts in British university budgets is that the British are too ready to accept the global sum allocated for higher education and that political action should have been instigated earlier, aimed at where the global decisions are actually made, in the Treasury, rather than post hoc, aimed at the DES. Not only do major US universities have their lobbyist within the state legislature, where the President and other senior officials will expect over the year to spend a good part of their time, but they also have links with Washington, where their professional associations, notably the American Council of Education (ACE), the Association of American Universities (AAU) and the National Association of College and University Business Officers (NACUBO), have a watching brief to make representations over legislation or appropriations affecting universities passing through either House.

At the technical level too the universities have shown themselves to be inventive. The inadequacies of formula based systems designed for a period of expansion are fully recognized and elaborate proposals are being put forward to amend the criteria. Thus Wisconsin after a two-year hiatus in formula funding has agreed a new formula with its state which provides that enrolments in any given year should be funded on the basis of the average of the previous two years, the current year's actuals, and forecasts for the next two years, so as to smooth over sharp fluctuations. In addition it has developed a new formula which identifies fixed as well as variable costs so as to reduce the damaging effects of enrolment decline. If the funding guidelines are exceeded a planning process is triggered for assessing the need to consolidate academic programmes and close facilities.[11] Ohio has followed a similar route; five priority expenditure components having been identified; departmental instruction and research, academic support, student services, administration, and plant operation and maintenance. The percentage of costs that are fixed are weighted by the share of the budget they compose. Simulations suggest that under this formula a typical Ohio state university would be able to protect 70-75% of budget if enrolments fell by 40%.[12]

'Faced with funding reductions proportional to enrolment declines,' writes Dr Gross, 'the temptations to take drastic measures to avoid the dreaded "financial exigency" process will intensify in the 1980's,'[13] and the fear is that it will promote practices which the Carnegie Council has termed 'ethically dubious if not illegal'. These include:

a   The proliferation of off-campus programmes of dubious quality
b   The lowering of admission and retention standards
c   'Hucksterism' in the recruitment of non-traditional and foreign students
d   The deliberate recruitment and admission of students lacking basic skills
e   Grade inflation and the lowering of academic standards[14]

The problems of budgetary constraint cannot necessarily be dealt with by tinkering with formulae. In the western and southern states, where demographic factors are relatively favourable, Proposition 13-type referenda to limit property taxes are rife. In many other states the inflation-recession squeeze has simply reduced state revenues available for higher education. In addition, with enrolment declines universities find themselves in many cases substantially over-built. Since buildings are funded on bond issues or loans the financial consequences in a period of high interest rates can be exceptionally severe. As a result universities are thrown back increasingly on their own resources and innovative skills to maintain their position. In any comparison with Britain one is immediately struck by the variety of sources of funds open to the US university and the energy which is expended at departmental as well as presidential level to maximize them. Alumni gifts, provision of public services, contract research, federal research support, externally funded programmes of all kinds and fee income can represent a very considerable alleviation of the effects of cuts in funds from public sources. In addition, the lack of a national salary and fee structure gives much greater flexibility in adjusting expenditure and income to local circumstances.

In the US university, unlike the British, resource allocation does not come together to be undertaken irrevocably by one body but is spread through the institution. The budget request cycle represents only one element, albeit an important element, in the funding process and if departments are cut there, or fail to achieve the additional resources they require, then they turn to external sources, to foundations, to state and federal agencies, to corporations and financial institutions to make up the difference. It is a truism of US academic life that if you fail to obtain funds from one source you try another, if you fail at State House you try Washington, and if you fail at one federal agency you try another. Not only are there more funding points than in Britain but there are also more points where political pressure can be applied. In comparison with Britain there is a much greater tolerance of uncertainty, a readiness, for example, to support tenured staff on soft money in the expectation that the funds will be renewed either from their original or some other source, and staff accept that a proportion of their salary may depend on the extent to which they can achieve external support. When Stanford's Operating Budget Guidelines suggests that Deans and chairmen of departments are the best qualified persons to examine and determine trade-offs in regard to individual programmes it is no more than describing in the particular the more fluid and open approach to funding which obtains in the US university system as a whole.

The uncertainty of funding at state level and the multiplicity of other funding sources in the US can sometimes combine to produce sudden and very sharp reductions in income. US universities have become used to coping with sudden financial cutbacks and their experience is relevant to the British situation. In New York State in 1975/76 exceptionally severe cuts were imposed on the university system and the experience on individual campuses of the State University of New York (SUNY) system suggested two generally applicable principles for such situations:

a   Make cuts to the level of half what you have been asked to make and then seek to negotiate your institution out of the other half.
b   Make your cuts quickly

The typical process in managing the cut was that the President handled the external negotiation while the Academic Vice-President took responsibility for imposing the cuts internally. The Academic Vice-President, in consultation with whatever internal group he set up, would lay down criteria against which individual academic programmes would be judged. At SUNY Brockport, for example, the criteria were:

Compatibility with institutional mission
Relevance to societal needs
Student demand
Productivity
Cost-effectiveness
Quality

At Brockport they took as operational principles openness of data, careful analysis, simplicity of the calculations involved, and negotiation rather than fiat. They turned over almost the entire administration to the cuts exercise, concentrated on that to the exclusion of anything else, and completed the process in two weeks.[15]

At the University of Michigan in 1980/81 the state imposed a 15% across-the-board budget cut. Here the President set up an administrative staff team to identify possible cuts of up to twice the size necessary and then set up academic committees, to each of which a member of the administrative staff team was assigned, to advise the Academic Vice-President, who was chairman of the budget committee, on how much of the cut should fall on their area. This process took longer than that described at Brockway but was similarly effective.[16]

In both these examples the state legislature imposed a cut and the institutions carried them out. In Tennessee, however, an alternative model has been developed. Legislatures in the US traditionally concern themselves mainly with budgetary and enrolment factors and leave the assessment of quality to the institutions themselves. In Tennessee, however, the Tennessee Higher Education Commission has developed a performance funding approach which relies heavily on the evaluation and self-evaluation of each institution's academic programmes, awarding points for numbers of programmes accredited, for student performance and for peer assessment, but which gives 20% of the points to assessment by students, recent graduates, members of the community and employers. Good and bad performance in these tests can be rewarded or penalized by an addition of up to 2% of an institution's budget or a reduction by up to the same amount.

The Tennessee process is unusual and is being watched closely by other states. What it reflects most clearly is the increasing desire for public accountability in higher education and a sense that there is a need to take more positive steps to reward quality. Perhaps the most common method of directing resources towards high quality programmes at the expense of others is the extensive system of programme review. Generally this is used more as a mechanism to evaluate graduate programmes, though in California its extension to undergraduate courses is also being discussed. In some states like New York, programme review conducted under state auspices is a mandatory part of the control systems erected by the state and its officials. An examination of the effectiveness of such an approach does not, however, suggest that programme review has contributed very much as yet to deciding where reductions in expenditure can be made.

The difficulty so often in US higher education is that cuts have to be made mid-year to meet a budget crisis. In 1982, for example, Ohio State University was required to reduce expenditure by $19.6m over six months and the University of Minnesota by $26m. Necessarily the mechanisms which must be employed in this situation will lay emphasis on the need for rapid adjustment and while alternative sources of income exist much more readily than in Britain, and universities and departments are more energetic in seeking them out, the continuous pressure on university budgets has taken its toll. More than 40% of full-time academic staff are now unionized and collective bargaining has become a new feature of many campuses, with the consequent inhibition in some institutions of academic participation in resource allocation.The proportion of part-time to full-time academic staff has dramatically increased from 23% in 1970 to around 50% ten years later, to the probable detriment of teaching standards. Decision-making has become increasingly centralized, bureaucratized, and 'technocratic', and research minded academics have become less willing to play a positive role in academic governance. Moreover, the pressure to raise external funds and the inherently more political style of university management have led to an increase in the power that external pressure groups, funding agencies, alumni and other private donors may exercise in resource allocation. Thus difficult resource decisions are becoming more difficult to take. At the state level there have been many examples, in New York, in Wisconsin and elsewhere, where universities or co-ordinating commissions have wished to close down whole campuses and redistribute the funds to high quality programmes on the flagship campuses but have been prevented from doing so by their legislatures. At the campus level multiple vetos in the decision-making system can prevent or at any rate slow down the process, so that it is difficult if not impossible to plan for retrenchment well in advance.

Any comparison between British and US higher education and their separate approaches to resource allocation at system or institutional level produces a number of paradoxes:

1   Although the US funding situation looks intrinsically less secure and more politicized than Britain's, British universities are more vulnerable to the whims as paymaster of the DES or the Government of the day because, having derived such a high proportion of their funds from one source (the UGC) for so long, they have not developed an entrepreneurial approach to funding.

2   The US system seems more authoritarian and to give less autonomy and protection to institutions because of the direct involvement of so many external bodies from the Governor's office through the legislature's staff and the co-ordinating commission down to the Board of Regents or Trustees. In fact the presence of so many different pressures often cancels on or another out, and no individual state has taken such draconian measures as the widespread college closures in Britain in the 1974 to 1978 period or the establishment of full cost fees for overseas students in 1979.

3   The US system of delegating power of decision to university officers, the President, the Vice-Presidents and as far down as Deans, might seem to establish an autocratic mode of governance, but in fact their formal authority is balanced by the power of an academic committee structure, whose advisory powers are on occasion decisive. But overarching this structure is a Board of lay Regents or Trustees,

in whom the final legal power to make decisions is vested. Britain places decision-making responsibility in a committee system involving at different levels both lay and academic interests. This has the advantage of legitimizing decisions, and of binding more constituents into the decision-making process. On the other hand when resources are tight, or when budgetary decisions are needed quickly, it can be cumbersome and indecisive.

4   The US system taken as a whole seems more fluid, flexible and open, it has more political pressure points and as a system is much more political and more politicized. At the same time it can also be less susceptible to sharp changes of policy because the extensive range of political pressures can cancel one another out, and the number of points in the decision-making process at which vetos can be exercised can inhibit adaptation to new circumstances. There is some evidence therefore that it may be less vulnerable to externally imposed change than the British system. In Britain, although the decision-making process seems designed to maintain the status quo, the almost total dependence on UGC funding and the absolute dependence of the UGC on government funding gives external authority a powerful lever to produce a change in priorities if Government chooses to use it.

Only one British institution of higher education, the Cranfield Institute of Technology, shares in any significant way some of the characteristics of the US university in terms of budgetary and resource allocation. For historical reasons Cranfield is funded on a different basis from universities, or indeed from polytechnics and colleges of higher education, and receives its money direct from the DES and not through the UGC. We have devoted a separate chapter (Chapter 13) to the Cranfield approach to resource allocation which we think offers a number of provocative comparisons with normal practice in universities.

There are conclusions to be drawn from a study of the US university scene which have relevance in Britain, and these are discussed in some detail in Chapter 14. Two impressions, however, ought to be conveyed here which have a tangential bearing on resource allocation. The first is that a strength of the US higher education system is its diversity and its ability to manage that diversity without reducing it by the imposition of financial or bureaucratic straight jackets. The second is the relentless openness of decision-making and particularly of the statistical bases of decision-making. We have referred frequently to the importance which British universities place on ensuring that the data base for decisions on resource allocation is widely circulated around departments and we believe that some further move in this direction by the UGC would be helpful.

NOTES AND REFERENCES

1 National Centre for Educational Statistics (1979) *Digest of Educational Statistics* Table 123

2 Gross, F.M. (1979) Formula budgeting and the financing of public higher education: panacea or nemesis for the 1980s *The AIR Professional File* 3

3 Millet, J.D. (1974) *The Budget Formula as the Basis for State Appropriations in Support of Higher Education* pp. 11-12. New York: Management Division, Academy for Academic Development. Quoted in F.M. Gross

4 Ladd, E.C. Jr. and Lipsett, S.M. (1979) How professors rated faculties in nineteen fields *Chronicle of Higher Education* 15 January pp.17,18. Quoted in F.M. Gross

5 For a more detailed account see Cornithus, J. Kent and Orwig, M. (1979) *Budgeting in Higher Education* AAHE — ERIC Higher Education Report No. 3, pp. 60-74

6 *AAUP Bulletin* 62 (December 1976)

7 Stanford University (1981) *Operating Budget Guidelines 1981/82* p. 9

8 Stanford University op.cit. p. 8

9 Stanford University op.cit. p. 4

10 See Scott, R.A. (1978) The hidden costs of government regulations *Change* April pp. 17-23

11 Fixed/variable cost analysis in the University of Wisconsin System Discussion Paper, November 1980

12 Hyde, W. (1981) *State Fiscal Constraints in Higher Education* p. 5. Working Papers in Education Finance, No. 33. Education Commission of the States

13 Gross, F.J. op.cit. p. 4

14 Scully, M. (1979) *The Chronicle of Higher Education* April. Quoted in F.M. Gross

15 Reported at UK/US Resource Allocation Conference, July 1981

16 Reported at UK/US Resource Allocation Conference, July 1981

RESOURCE ALLOCATION
IN THE CRANFIELD INSTITUTE OF TECHNOLOGY

The Cranfield Institute of Technology has a resource allocation system unique in British higher education. In many ways it is also unique as an institution. Our purpose in including a chapter describing its procedures is not to suggest that they could be widely copied within the university system, but to present a different and original approach to the problems of equity and efficiency in resource allocation. The Institute grew out of the former College of Aeronautics and is the only educational institution in Britain that has an airfield from which it derives an income. Unlike the universities covered in this study it does not come under the aegis of the UGC but is directly funded by the DES. Student numbers in 1979/80 and 1981/2 were as follows:

	Home		Overseas		Total	
	79/80	81/82	79/80	81/82	79/80	81/82
Postgraduate	748	918	356	387	904	1305
Undergraduate	120	106	16	17	136	123
	868	1024	372	404	1040	1428
Short Course FTE						374

In 1979-80 Cranfield had 316 academic and related staff and 257 technical and support staff (of whom 176 were on 'open ended appointments' and the remainder on limited term). In 1981-82 the figures were 362 academic and related and 239 technical and support staff. Subject interests are restricted to technology, science and management.

Cranfield has a Court, Council, Senate and five Faculties on a traditional university model, but the key committee is a body advisory to the Vice-Chancellor called the Vice-Chancellor's Committee, which comprises all heads of department. Heads of department are appointed by a joint committee of Council and Senate for periods of five years. They are in a very real sense managers of their departments, which are given the maximum degree of autonomy, academic and financial. The Vice-Chancellor's Committee agrees a unit cost for each department, a figure which comprises each department's own direct costs, departmental overheads and Institute overheads. Each department bids for a student number allocation and is awarded a target which is then multiplied by the unit cost, less the anticipated fee income, to provide a departmental allocation.

Unit costs make provision for the following elements:

Academic Staff
Supporting staff
Space
Equipment
Supplies and services
Contributions

In calculating individual unit costs, the following principles are used:

For academic staff: the same figure per student is applied to every subject. This figure is determined by applying an agreed salary point on a given staff/student ratio.

For supporting staff: each subject area is assessed separately under this heading, according to the nature of the subject. First, a qualitative assessment is made of the nature of staff required — for example some subjects require a high level of technical support, while others require only clerical support. Secondly, an assessment is made of the appropriate staff/student ratio for each subject.

For space: there is an agreed area per student for each subject. This is converted into a figure per student when the floor area charge for the year is determined. A software student requires less floor area than a hardware student, and this is reflected in the relative unit costs.

For equipment: each subject area's equipment needs are assessed and converted into a cost per student; this will obviously vary according to the nature of the subject.

For supplies and services: the principles are the same as for equipment.

Contributions: for unit cost purposes, these are calculated as a percentage of the agreed salary costs of each unit cost.

Thus, each subject area has its own unit cost. These are agreed annually in advance, and modifications are made only with the agreement of all other heads of department.

Once the unit costs for the year are established, it becomes possible to determine how many students can be funded in each subject area. Departments make their bids in line with their own departmental policy. The Vice-Chancellor's Committee then allocates agreed targets for each department in the light of the funds likely to be available. Departments are paid according to the students they actually recruit up to their target figure. If they exceed their targets they are paid in proportion to any funds released by virtue of other departments failing to achieve their targets.

The overall academic balance of the Institute is thus achieved, in the end, by market forces. A head of department can deliberately choose to restrict recruitment if he considers that his department can continue to operate on a reasonable financial basis with the reduced grant. On the other hand, a department may wish to risk exceeding its targets in the hope that additional funds will become available from other departments' under-achievement.

One feature of the unit costs system which is currently under active review is whether or not to introduce some recognition of economies of scale. At the moment achievement up to the target figure is paid on a flat rate basis. This has the advantage of encouraging growth (as long as it can be financed from the DES grant) but does not necessarily encourage economies of scale as a department grows.

The DES grant, however, contributes to only a proportion of Cranfield's expenditure.

TABLE 22

Total recurrent income to Cranfield Institute of Technology 1979/80 — 1981/82

	1979/80		1981/82	
	£m	%	£M	%
DES recurrent funds	5.84	(34.4)	6.94	(29.6)
Tuition fees (including short course fees, and fees from non-EC students)	2.51	(14.8)	5.03	(21.5)
Sponsored research and development	5.99	(35.3)	7.77	(33.2)
Residential charges	1.74	(10.2)	2.26	(9.6)
Miscellaneous recurrent income	0.27	(1.6)	0.36	(1.5)
Capital grant	0.36	(2.1)	0.79	(3.4)
New capital loans	0.28	(1.6)	0.29	(1.2)
	£16.99	(100.0%)	£23.41	(100.0%)

A comparison between 1976-7 and 1981-2 shows that the proportion of Cranfield's income from DES recurrent funds has fallen from 44.4% to 29.6% but that income from tuition fees has risen from 9.2% to 21.5% and from sponsored research and development from 27.3% to 33.2%.

There has been a significant increase in the proportion of support from non-DES sources; to a certain extent this has been influenced by an increase in overseas tuition fees and the phasing in of full fees for non-EC students but, even allowing for these factors, the success in generating an alternative resource base has been considerable. In 1976-7 Cranfield depended on DES funding to the extent of just over 50%, in 1981-2 its dependence was reduced to less than 35%.

An analysis of Cranfield's resource-base shows the following:

DES recurrent grant is based largely on the Institute's total UK and EC student activity. To enable the DES to assess the level of grant, a co-ordinated overall academic plan for the development of UK and EC student activity is prepared on a five-year rolling basis, updated annually. The plan takes account of the individual policies and plans of each department.

Tuition fees are derived from individual students who enrol in particular departments and units. Effectively the income from tuition fees is based on efforts to attract students at the departmental level.

Sponsored research and development income is generated largely at the departmental level; central involvement is only needed to ensure that the basic facilities required are available for the departments.

Residential income is a function of the efficient local management of residences.

Capital income depends upon a combination of departmental and central effort; the initial impetus or demand generally comes from the departmental level but, because of the complexity of raising and managing such resources, a central co-ordinating function is necessary.

The operations of individual departments are vital in the Cranfield system. The style of operations can most easily be described by considering some specific examples. Two very different departments will serve to illustrate the departmental resource model.

The Cranfield School of Management is primarily a teaching school, with major programmes in degree courses and short courses. The College of Aeronautics (which operates as a department), on the other hand, operates in the field of advanced technology with a mixed programme of activities which includes a large element of externally sponsored research and development.

The 1981/82 income for the two departments is given in Table 23 (figures are in £000).

TABLE 23
Total recurrent income to Cranfield Institute of Technology, departments of management and aeronautics 1981/82

	Management £000	Aeronautics £000
Central allocation	947	1,286
Long course tuition fees	300	397
Short course tuition fees	1,040	186
Sponsored R & D	170	1,835
Miscellaneous external	55	35
Internal services	10	11
	2,522	3,750

The central allocation to each department is based on UK and EC student numbers and the 'unit cost' for such students in that department.

The level of UK and EC tuition fees is set nationally. The level of non-EC degree course tuition fees is agreed across the Institute as a percentage of the agreed unit cost in each area. Thus a non-EC student in one department will not pay the same fee as in another; however, they will both pay the same proportion of the estimated cost of the education provided.

The level of short course fees is set to recover the actual cost of providing such courses, as assessed by the unit cost system. It should be noted that short courses are assessed on a full not a marginal cost basis.

In the case of the two departments given above, the agreed unit costs in Management are about 55% of those in Aeronautics; the difference in unit costs lies in the expensive laboratory requirements of Aeronautics. It can be seen from the figures that educational income in Management (ie central income plus fees) is about £2.3m, while in Aeronautics it is about £1.9m. However, in student number terms Management has about 50% more students.

The total income for sponsored research and development activities is credited wholly to the department earning that income. Cranfield policy is that the full costs of all research and development work, including overheads, must be met from R & D income. Thus, a department wishing to undertake a significant amount of research council work, where no overheads may be available, will have to attract additional compensating overheads from industrial sources.

In the case of the two departments shown above, Aeronautics carries out an extensive R & D programme; in financial terms it represents about half the activity. On the other hand, Management's sponsored programme is relatively small. Departments also derive certain miscellaneous income from other services, both external and internal.

The 1981/82 expenditure accounts for both departments are shown in Table 24.

TABLE 24
Total expenditure in Cranfield Institute of Technology, departments of management and aeronautics 1981/82

	Management £000	Aeronautics £000
Academic staff salaries	736	430
Supporting staff salaries	280	270
Sponsored staff salaries	78	1,111
Visiting staff	110	40
Departmental supplies, services and equipment	738	745
Sponsored supplies, services and equipment	50	357
Estates, rate and utilities	105	255
Contributions	248	278
	2,345	3,486

Each head of department is entitled to utilize departmental resources in any way he wishes within the generally agreed framework, provided the resultant overall balance at the end of the year is acceptable. Balances are carried forward to the following year; in general most departments attempt to carry forward a small working surplus, and any planned deficits have to be approved by the Institute beforehand.

No department has a centrally approved staffing establishment. It is left entirely to the head of department to decide on the appropriate level of staffing in each category; appointments, however, must be made by the proper appointing procedure, and must be made within the approved scales. No senior/junior ratios are applied, and appointments to senior posts are considered on merit. Each head of department is free to decide how much to spend on 'Supplies, Services and Equipment'. No specific proportion of funds is set for equipment purposes, and Cranfield itself receives no earmarked equipment funds. The overall cost of 'Estates, Rates and Utilities' is agreed annually in advance and then expressed as a charge per square metre of space occupied. If a department increases or reduces its space then its resultant charge for estates, rates and utilities is adjusted accordingly. The 'Contributions' figure represents the cost of essential central services, such as the library or central administration which cannot be financed on an 'as-used' basis. The total contribution figure is agreed annually in advance and expressed as a percentage of salaries and of working capital. Thus an individual department can reduce its liability for contribution by reducing its salary expenditure or by operating with a reduced working capital requirement. Those central services which are funded from the contributions must live within the resultant budgets; if there is a decline in Cranfield's operating activity (as reflected in total salaries expenditure), or trading position (as reflected in working capital requirements), the central services must also adjust their affairs accordingly. The computing service receives only 40% of its total costs from mandatory departmental contributions and must make up the remainder by charging departments and other users for services rendered.

As many central services as possible are managed on a 'contractual' basis — that is, their services are paid for on an as-used basis with user departments having the freedom to obtain the service elsewhere, possibly from outside. This is done to encourage the service areas to operate competitively.

In the case of the two departments given above, it can be seen that staff expenditure in Aeronautics is about 50% higher than in Management. This does not necessarily mean more staff, but may also mean a higher average salary because of the nature of the staff. Moreover, staff can be given incentive payments, particularly where income generation is involved, and only payments of more than £750 need to be notified centrally. On the supplies and services budget head, Aeronautics expenditure is significantly higher, as would be expected; the department also occupies more space than Management. Overall, both departments are in surplus on the year; however, one department brought forward a deficit from the previous year, while the other plans a deficit for the following year. In both cases these financial plans have to receive the approval of the Institute beforehand. If deficits grow on an unplanned basis, this is brought to the wider attention of the Institute; normally this can be corrected by discussion and consequential action. In the last five years or so two departments have been closed and the staff re-deployed because of growing signs of financial insolvency.

On the capital side Cranfield also operates an unusual system for funding capital development which cannot be covered by the DES grant. First, Cranfield includes in the space charge payable by all departments a capital levy which is credited to the building development fund. Every activity contributes, including service areas and residences. Second, it borrows money as and when required. In addition, it attracts earmarked support for specific projects from other sources where possible.

Table 25 gives details of the building development fund for 1981/82 (£000):

TABLE 25
Income and expenditure on capital projects, Cranfield Institute of Technology 1981/82

	£000	%
INCOME		
Capital grants	793	(46%)
Space charges	672	(39%)
New loans	259	(15%)
	1,723	(100%)
EXPENDITURE		
Major projects	1,169	(68%)
Minor projects	391	(23%)
Existing loan charges	163	(9%)
	1,723	(100%)

As Cranfield continues to develop, the balance of the building development fund will change. However, it should be noted that all activities contribute to the capital development of the Institute, through the floor area charge. In this way, the full costs of the Institute's development is passed on to the users of its various services.

Cranfield claims the following characteristics for the system:

1 It encourages departmental autonomy and clarification of departmental objectives. Departments must be outward looking to survive, since there is no help to be obtained from within the Institute.

2 It encourages diversity of activity.

3 There are few central constraints on departments. Associated with this characteristic is the assumption that managers and heads of department are capable of positive management.

4 The system enables departments (and thus the Institute) to respond quickly to external factors.

5 The system makes *internal* assessments of departmental activities primarily on a resource basis, not on an academic basis. For this reason it is essential to have strong *external* assessments of standards — in academic terms the role of external examiners becomes even more important, while the very fact that research and development funds are obtained on an *externally* assessed basis is essential.

6   The system tends to benefit larger departments who, because of their size, have greater freedom to switch resources. Smaller departments have to be nursed very carefully in the early stages.

The success of the Cranfield approach is striking in terms of income generation. In 1970/71 DES income made up 80% of its income and in 1981/82 about 35%. By comparison the average for the university system in 1979/80 was about 77%. But it should be remembered that in academic profile Cranfield is distinctly atypical of institutions in the university system. It has no arts, only a very few undergraduates (all located on the former National College of Aeronautical Engineering campus, some eleven miles away), and has restricted its range of interests to those where there is a market. The Cranfield model illustrates a number of principles which constantly recur in considering traditional university resource allocation systems. In particular it provides evidence that, in its own special case, it is possible to develop an institution on a market-led basis, that it is possible for an institution to operate with an entirely devolved financial system where departmental autonomy is extended to the very limit, and that, given certain inherent advantages combined with the institutional will to do it, it is possible to finance academic development on the back of earned income. It is important always to keep in mind that Cranfield is a special case amongst institutions of higher education in Britain and that its functions are different from those of a university. A full assessment of the success of its approach to internal organization and any proper comparison with the traditional university model would have to include a review of its effect on academic development.

NOTE
1   Much of the data reproduced in this chapter is drawn from *The Management of Resources at Cranfield Institute of Technology*, a paper given by M.D. Geddes and A.J.J. Davies to the Programme of Institutional Management in Higher Education, Workshops on Managing Basic Units, Paris 1982.

MANAGING THE CUTS 1981/82

In the previous chapters we have described the resource allocation machinery in universities in the period of expansion and 'level funding'. The government decision announced in the March 1981 Expenditure White Paper to reduce university recurrent grants by 8½% by 1983/84, and the subsequent issue of the UGC's grant allocation letter of 1 July 1981 propelled the universities into a period of retrenchment and contraction. Under present government policy once the 'volume cuts' have been achieved by 1983/84 the university sector may expect a period of level funding but the national economic prospects, together with the contraction of the number of 18-year-olds, make it difficult to be optimistic about the future funding of the university sector of higher education. This will place a premium on universities' ability to reallocate resources within a fixed or, more likely, a decreasing budget.

We therefore undertook an exercise to discover how effectively a cross-section of universities had been able to re-allocate resources within the reduced budgets available for 1981/82, 1982/83 and 1983/84. The eleven universities selected included two technological universities, four civic universities and five new universities. These ranged in size from just over 9,000 home and EC students to just over 2,000, and included four medium size institutions of between 4,500 and 3,500. For convenience we will identify the universities by the letters A to K. The effect of the cuts was varied. In terms of student targets they ranged from an addition of 2% between 1979/80 and 1983/84 and a cut of 30%, with four of the other universities suffering reductions of less than 2% though with changes in the mix of students within the overall targets. In terms of recurrent finance the cuts covered a range from one of 2% to one of 41%.

There was no observable pattern in the effects of the cuts in student numbers on particular kinds of universities, except that the four civics seem as a class to have suffered less than the rest on the basis of a simple comparison between 1979/80 figures and 1983/84. This generalization like many others is dangerous because it conceals considerable variations in universities' particular circmstances. All the civic universities in this group, for example, had medical schools so that the effect of the UGC's policy of restricting the expansion of medical school intakes rather than actually reducing the numbers had a distorting effect on comparisons of student target reductions and on the recurrent financial savings which had to be achieved to compensate for the relative protection accorded to medical education. Again, simple comparisons of published data ignore variations in the age of buildings and the cost of the premises budget generally, the expected rate of retirement of staff, the extent of universities' dependence on overseas student fee income and the burden of academic or other commitments. Comparative data on total student numbers and recurrent grant were therefore unreliable guides to the extent to which universities had to re-allocate their resources in the new situation.

An important consideration in reviewing universities' ability to cope with enforced retrenchment was the extent to which they had undertaken previous reallocation exercises or had managed their affairs in such a way as to be able to limit the damage that the July letter might cause. From 1979 onwards all the universities were taking an increasingly stringent attitude in filling vacancies and very few were actually creating any new posts. The position was by no means uniform however. Two of the new universities had undertaken significant and formalized cost-cutting exercises in the 1974/75 period which clearly stood them in good stead in 1981/82. In one of these universities special machinery had been set up to carry out a short-term exercise but in the other a resources committee set up at that time had become the key piece of machinery for resource allocation and had established a reputation in the university for tough but fair decisions. Five universities embarked on special savings exercises in 1979. One large civic decided in November 1979 to seek savings at the rate of £800K from the recurrent expenditure by September 1982 (out of annual expenditure of around £45m) but in January 1981, even though the savings were on target, up-rated the programme to seek savings of £1.62m at 1979 prices by July 1982. Another aimed at saving £1m over two years from November 1979 and had reached £900K by July 1981. A third established a target of £800K. Two of the new universities established special programmes which inter alia reviewed their academic operations (not the two which had had formal savings exercises in the mid-1970s). One set up a special committee, the other used a sub-committee of its development committee, but in both cases their reports failed to gain Senate approval, prior to the July letter. In one of these cases, however, the report proved to be an important strategic exercise for the university and the recommendations were in effect re-considered and largely adopted by the Senate in the discussions post-July 1981. Even though every university adopted a vacancy freezing policy with varying degrees of stringency from 1979, and some universities opted for complete moratoria for some periods, four of the new universities needed to establish some wholly new posts in this period, either to reflect expansion agreed with the UGC in particular subject areas or to seek some change in balance within the institution.

Universities were thus in varying stages of preparedness when the July letter reached them. They were not, however, assisted in this process by two difficulties arising from UGC policy. The first was the practice, described more fully in Chapter 3, of UGC disbursements late in the financial year to compensate for inflation. The unpredictability of these funds and their arrival at the end of a year of considerable austerity was in some universities seen as a contradiction of policies adopted earlier in the year. There can be no doubt that they reduced the enthusiasm of academics for cost-saving exercises and in the case of one of the two new universities, which embarked on an academic review exercise, they appear to have played a part in the Senate's rejection of the university's pre-July 1981 'restructuring' plan. A second feature was the UGC's adoption of 1979/80 as its base for decisions rather than 1980/81. The continued pressure of applications for undergraduate admission, arising from the size of the 18-year-old age group, meant that even in a period of 'level funding' universities found it hard to control their admissions targets, with the result that university populations grew by 1 or 2% in almost all universities and by as much as 3% in two of them between 1979/80 and 1980/81. The position was exacerbated by a swing back to science amongst applicants, with the result that in some universities the UGC's proposed expanded target for science and technology numbers by 1983/84 had already been met by 1981/82, with a consequential decrease in unit costs. As a result, eight of the eleven universities had to impose more severe reductions on student targets than were implied by the simple comparison between 1979/80 and 1983/84 targets presented in the UGC letters. Inevitably this fuelled a suspicion that the UGC was basing its decisions on inadequate or out-of-date information and rendered internal decision-making that much more difficult.

The reallocation problems caused by the July letter cannot be described by reference to overall percentage reductions but depend acutely on individual institutional circumstances. Technological university A, for example, which had been able to convince the UGC that it had been under-funded for some years, suffered a minimal reduction in income and has had to undertake no significant reallocation exercise. Technological university B, however, was required to reduce its student numbers by 30% and needed to reduce expenditure by £6.35m. In consequence it had to undertake the most major restructuring exercise that any British university has been faced with. The four civic universities were also set considerable problems because of their size, subject mix and liability to high expenditure on premises items. The largest of the group, D, found itself needing to reduce expenditure by £4.6m (around 10% of total expenditure); the second largest, C, by £2.663m by July 1982 or at least £2.857m by July 1983 (4.7% and 5.1% of total expenditure respectively); the next largest, E, by £5m (a reduction of 11.6%); and the fourth, F, by a figure which it prefers to describe as 13% over the period 1979/80 to 1983/84 rather than as a cash figure. Of the new universities, university J faced the need to reduce expenditure by £3.73m or 22%; university G by £2.1m or 12.5% (at 1981/82 prices); university I by £1.74m (at 1981/82 prices) or 11.1%; university H by £1.4m or 15%; and university K by £1.4m or

7.4% (at 1980/81 prices).

The average industrialist looking at these figures would perhaps not be impressed by the difficulties they posed in slimming down the various institutions but this would be to ignore the fact that 75% of university income is consumed by salaries and wages and 40% by academic and academic related salaries, 90% of which are paid to staff on tenure. Moreover, universities work under two important constraints. The academic staff must themselves take or participate in the crucial decisions at Senate and Council; and the universities themselves, as teaching institutions with responsibilities to students, cannot face closure for a period or, put another way, need to secure sufficient consent from their non-academic staff so as to avoid strike action. The extent to which salaries and wages dominate university expenditure dictated the basic strategy of freezing vacancies which all universities adopted to a greater or lesser extent from 1979 onwards.

Within this strategy there were many different approaches. University D needed to reduce student numbers in arts-based subjects by nearly 8% and increase them in medicine by nearly 12% and science by 2%. It broadly accepted the UGC's student targets and decided to seek the financial savings by a 6% across-the-board cut in 1982/83 (£2.7m) and a selective cut of £1.9m to operate from 1983/84. 75% of the savings were achieved in the first phase from academic and academic related posts, and 15-20% from non-academic posts leaving only a very small proportion from non-staff related costs. University C had to reduce arts student numbers by 6%, and science by 3% (though the UGC had scheduled it for a 2% increase which it had already exceeded by 1981/82), whilst increasing medicine by 12%. It accepted these targets and imposed cuts pro-rata, but planned to achieve 30% of its reduction from the non-academic sector of the university including staffing, fuel, telephones, maintenance and other items in the premises budget. University E approached the problem rather differently, deciding to reduce its staff/student ratio from 8.3:1 to 9.45:1 requiring a loss of 143 academic and academic related posts, reducing its ratio of academic to secretarial staff from 4.8:1 to 5.2:1, a loss of 50 posts, but retaining a 1:1 ratio of academic to technician posts in the sciences, a loss of 90 posts. In addition £250K was cut from the £2.9m allocated for departmental grants. This university, however, had significant non-UGC reserves and it has been proposed that reserves and unencumbered investment income should be used to spread the contraction to 1985.

The group of new universities followed slightly different strategies. University J, which had the most severe cut of the group, opted for considerations relating to the academic shape of the institution, but within that sought to reduce academic posts by around 100 between October 1980 and October 1983. A 20% across-the-board cut was agreed except for 45% for the social and welfare side of the university and 14% on premises, with the portering establishment to be reduced by 40%. At university G the resources committee reviewed the university and recommended selective cuts. University I largely put into effect the report previously submitted to its Senate and planned to reduce academic staff from 480 to 410 using transfers to other universities and secondments in addition to natural wastage and early retirement. Departmental allocations were cut by 12% and central services, academic and non-academic by 8%. University K aimed to save between 35 and 46 academic posts but looked to income generation significantly to reduce the need to make reductions.

University B deserves separate attention because the scale of the loss of income it suffered demanded a more intensive exercise than in any other university. If no change had occurred in staff and student numbers the university would have faced deficits of £2m in 1981/82, £4.55m in 1982/83 and £6.35m in 1983/84. Action therefore had to be taken quickly and the anticipated deficit in 1981/82 was reduced immediately by £1.2m by decisions to cancel minor works, major maintenance items and part-time teaching for the year. The university then adopted a six-stage programme to draw up an academic plan:

1 Determination of the total number of students
2 Determination of the student number split between arts and science
3 Determination of the future of departments and courses
4 Determination of the size of the support services
5 Determination of the future of any other activities within the academic sector
6 Determination of the deployment of resources necessary to support the re-shaped academic sector and the steps necessary to realize the plan

An essential feature of the realization of the plan was an invitation to all staff over the age of fifty to volunteer for early retirement. In the event the university adopted a plan for 3,000 students (250 more than suggested by the UGC) but with a 27:73 split of arts to science in line with UGC advice. On the resources side expenditure on the academic sector was to be reduced by 29.1% and on the non-academic sector by 32.2%. Academic staff/student ratios were to be reduced from 1:12 to 1:13.5 (arts) and from 1:11 to 1:12.5 (science) but the existing ratios of 0.85 technical to one academic post and one clerical/secretarial to six weighted academic posts were to be maintained. Within both academic and non-academic sectors harsh choices have had to be made.

Universities varied very greatly in the timescale within which they were able to complete their planning process. University B, for example, perhaps because its problems were so severe, set itself a timetable in August for completing its plan and obtaining approval from Senate and Council, together with concluding all its internal consultations with trades unions, departments and faculties, by 15 December, and achieved it. University K announced its required savings target, with the number of posts to be lost, within ten days of receipt of the July letter and completed its academic plan by 15 December. University I aimed to complete its plan by 14 December and in fact did so on 9 January 1982. Other universities took longer, either as a point of strategy — one university saw a positive advantage in not having a master plan — or simply because the procedures adopted involved lengthy consultations. University G, for example, relied on a review of all university activities by its resources committee which produced its report for university-wide discussion in March 1982 for decision in the summer term. It is clear that some universities were still discussing their plan well into the summer of 1982. While in some cases this may indicate an inability to take necessary decisions with proper effectiveness, it must not be taken to be true for all. University D, for example, imposed a pro-rata 6% cut on all departments and then set up a group to make selective additional cuts which in some cases led to a restoration of the 6%. Many universities in fact have a distinct style of decision-making which emphasizes a certain weighty deliberation above any need for speed. On the other hand the weaknesses, endemic in one or two institutions' resource allocation machinery, have been exposed for all to see.

It has often been postulated in the past that the structure of internal university governance and decision-making would be seriously altered if universities were ever required to take really harsh decisions affecting their own members. A review of how decisions were taken in these eleven universities would not, however, support this though it is fair to say that universities were in a sense let off the most difficult decisions by the establishment of the USS Early Retirement scheme which enabled all the institutions concerned to avoid the need to declare academic redundancies at least within twelve months of the July letter. The striking fact in so many cases is how the existing planning and resource allocation machinery stood up to the strain of the decisions required of it. In two universities, B and K, the split committee responsibilities for academic planning and resource allocation were brought together, in the former in joint meetings, in the latter in the form of a new joint committee, to give greater coherence to decision-making. In university I where a tough minded development committee had failed to convince Senate of the scale and implications of the savings needed in 1980, the committee's judgements on the July letter were monitored, or in effect refereed, by a joint working party of the committee and representatives of the boards of studies which in the end pronounced itself satisfied with the development committee's judgement of the extent and appropriate distribution of the required savings between main expenditure heads. There may be some evidence of a strengthening of the central authority in university C which empowered its Vice-Chancellor to decide which vacancies should be exempted from a general moratorium on posts and in university K where the finance and general purposes committee of Council must now approve the release of funds for any new or replacement post on the academic side. But set against this was the decision by university B, the worst hit of all the universities, to establish from the outset that 'to gain broad acceptance for the plan, staff had to be given an opportunity to participate in its formulation at every stage: no relevant information should be confined to any "inner" group and it should be demonstrated that constructive criticism could affect the nature of the outcome.' It might have been expected that in a cost-cutting exercise administrators would come to exercise proportionately more power than in the past but the evidence that emerges is that the pressure of timescales and difficult decisions has in fact had the effect of increasing the close working relationships in a number of universities between senior academics and senior administrators. Greater reliance has clearly been placed in many universities on small sub-committees of main resource allocation committees, but no university saw any fundamental shift in the committee structure or in the relationships between Council and Senate.

It is, of course, too early, only one year from the July letter, to judge finally how effectively universities have been able to retrench and re-deploy their resources. The difficulties of dirigiste decision-making at the institutional level, especially in the wake of a severe cost-cutting exercise, should not be underestimated. On the whole, universities seem to have followed UGC advice about the distribution of student numbers. Whether this was because it was good advice, or because it was thought politic to do so, or because no consensus emerged for any other decisions is not clear. At universities B, C, E and I academic departments have been closed or merged and at I the university explicitly used quality factors in taking its decisions. On the other hand many universities have engineered quite significant changes of budget distribution within overall university expenditure. Most universities have paid lip service to the need for income generation but, apart from in the field of overseas student fee income, only two universities, B and K, appear to have taken active steps as a matter of policy to achieve it and only K explicitly established a figure (£500K pa) which it was aiming at by 1983/84 and on which it was basing its plan. Only four universities have set up schemes where there are clear financial incentives for academic departments to attract overseas students.

What all this suggests is that the universities have probably coped reasonably well with the cost-saving imposed on them by the July 1981 letter. At least one university, B, has done much better than this and has shown a resolution and clear sightedness in the face of adversity worthy of permanent record. In contrast, another technological university (not one of the universities included in this exercise) which had cuts of a nearly similar level appears to have struggled throughout the year to reach agreement on what steps should be taken. But universities have shown comparatively little initiative and drive in seeking new sources of income and have often passed up the opportunity to make significant changes in their academic structure to build up the academic strengths required to compete in the new environment. There has, however, been no general disposition to sacrifice essential non-academic services like maintenance to preserve academic programmes. Universities with medical schools have faced particular problems of internal redistribution of resources and it is probably true that if the UGC had not sought protection for medical faculties they would have suffered equality of treatment with science and technology departments. Perhaps in the first year of the cuts it was right for universities to concentrate on finding the way to balance the books and avoid substantial deficits in the third year of the UGC's planning period when the cuts cumulatively are greatest, but such a policy is ultimately negative and liable to reinforce the run down of the universities which so many outside commentators have predicted.

In December 1982 the UGC published a letter to the Secretary of State entitled *The Restructuring of the University System: an interim appraisal.*[2] This paper tended to confirm some of our findings for the university system as a whole. The assessment emphasized the special problems faced by universities in making the required cuts at the speed necessary to meet the run-down in resources. They arose because of the long lead time required to terminate undergraduate courses and because:

'universities are self-regulating communities of scholars and all academic staff are members of the body corporate. The decision making processes are complex and depend on widespread consent. Even under the urgent pressure of reduced funding a realignment of academic priorities is not easy to achieve without considerable debate over a fairly long period.'[3]

The UGC could have added that part of the problem is that in practice academic priorities are extremely difficult to decide: subjects vary in their interest to sixth formers, to researchers and to Government almost from year to year and certainly over decades. Moreover the phasing out of some unfashionable or 'uneconomic' arts-based subjects can sometimes produce only imperceptible savings for disproportonate effort and disruption. The UGC's prime concern was rightly that the relief provided by early retirement might be misused by universities if they were undiscriminating in their acceptances of voluntary redundancies and ran down priority subjects simply to meet budgetary targets. The UGC estimated on the basis of figures then available that staff/student ratios would have moved as shown in Table 26 by 1984/85.

The UGC concluded its letter with the following statement:

'So far we believe that the university system is adapting itself to the new levels of funding broadly in accordance with the Committee's advice. However there are aspects which cause us anxiety and uncertainty remains.'[5]

TABLE 26
Staff/student ratios actual and anticipated by the UGC: GB Universities
1979/80 and 1984/85[4]

	1979/80	1984/85
Medicine	6:2	7:2
Dentistry	6:7	7:3
Engineering and technology	9:2	10:0
Biological sciences	8:8	9:2
Mathematical sciences	10:6	11:2
Physical sciences	7:4	8:8
Social studies	11:6	11:8
Arts	10:3	10:9

Our study would support this conclusion. We remain convinced, however, that if universities are to be assisted in reaching decisions on priorities for resource allocation the UGC has a positive and necessary contribution to make by revealing much more than it does now about the data which help to form its judgements and the range of criteria involved. Their evidence to the Select Committee on Education, Science and Arts and the assessment letter quoted above are useful in themselves but take us only a short way down the road of more open decision-making within the UGC.

NOTES AND REFERENCES
1   At the time of writing this decision remains the subject of correspondence with the UGC which has sought explanations from universities which appear to be in danger of overshooting their student number targets.
2   Letter from the chairman of the UGC to the Secretary of State dated 16 December 1982.
3   Op.cit. para. 12
4   Op.cit. para. 27
5   Op.cit. para. 35

LONGER-TERM PROSPECTS
FOR REALLOCATING RESOURCES

Conventional wisdom suggests that the present trends in university finance will continue: the screw will continue to be tightened, vacancies will continue not to be filled, and more and harsher economies will have to be made. It is very difficult to argue positively against the likelihood of this scenario: neither demography, the nation's finances nor the public mood would seem to offer support even for modest optimism. Moreover, the leaked Central Policy Review Staff memorandum putting forward the possibility of a higher education system entirely financed by tuition fees, themselves covered by loans rather than grants, suggests an even more radical change for the worse for many institutions.[1] We believe that we must accept that a pessimistic scenario, in terms of UGC financial support, is a more likely prospect than any other and that the university system needs to plan accordingly. Of course what is true for the system may not be true for individual institutions. Some may well benefit from the changes, while others might suffer disproportionately. Generalizations about the problems of resource re-allocation are therefore dangerous.

The evidence provided by our study suggests that in the short run universities proved themselves to be reasonably adaptable and flexible in the way they managed the cuts in 1981/82. There were variations even within the group of institutions studied. Not all could be said to have coped with similar ease, and some of the not so hard hit may have found themselves in more internal difficulties than those which suffered most. Outside our group of universities there is evidence of a minority of institutions having severe difficulties, but of the majority having coped fairly well. How far performance over the first year should be taken as indicative over the whole 1981-4 cuts period is difficult to say. We can cite particular examples of institutions in the university system as a whole which do not appear to be facing up to problems or taking decisive action at the right times but the same can be said of any large organization facing substantial reductions in income, whether in Government or in the public sector or in private industry. We do not, for example, think there is justification for the sweeping assertion by the chairman of Unilever, Dr Kenneth Durham, that:

'I gained the impression that our higher educational institutions have neither the organizational structures nor as yet the management skills to deal with what will be a difficult situation over the next few years.

Industrialists have had to learn how to manage change in difficult times and I hope the need for academics to do the same will be an important lesson from our seminar.'²

The record of British industry as a whole, if not Unilever, does not justify such an unfavourable comparison.

Nevertheless, there are few grounds for complacency and, if the future is as bleak as some predict, universities will have to change in many ways. In this respect we found the experience of US universities instructive and we drew the following general conclusions from it:

1   The US university seemed more reactive to its external environment and more responsive to market forces. The British system responded quickly to external negative constraints but was less inclined to react positively to new opportunities.

2   US universities, although they had a majority of full-time academic staff appointed on tenure, seemed to have found ways of adapting their circumstances to fit financial requirements without compromising irrevocably their tenure position. This was partly because of the financial exigency provisions in contracts of employment and partly because they were more entrepreneurial at a central and a departmental level in obtaining external income which could cover proportions of individual members of staff's salary costs and more inventive in an accounting sense in accepting these contributions as part of a continually fluctuating financial scene.

3   Although decisions were becoming more centralized in US universities because of the pressure of financial constraints, nevertheless departments and other budgetary units had more freedom and more enthusiasm for seeking alternative funding, and the higher education system seemed to throw up more alternative sources of funding than exist in Britain.

4   The US university was almost certainly more effective at 'crisis management' when sharp financial cuts had to be administered. There is an advantage in some circumstances in making retrenchment decisions quickly and decisively. The US university had machinery for doing this and if the internal authorities could not handle it, the Board of Regents or Trustees had the legal authority that was required. In Britain painful decisions were more difficult to take and the internal constitution of universities militated against speedy decision-making.

5   Both systems suffered from timing problems in resource allocation imposed by the fact that the procedures for settling the budget at state (in the US) or government level (in Britain) were complex and long drawn out. In neither case does there seem much likelihood of change so universities must adapt their own procedures accordingly

rather than persistently cling to the belief that next year the position will improve.

Only Cranfield among British institutions of higher education shared, to any significant extent, the organizational and decision-making characteristics of the US university. Indeed our US colleagues commented particularly on parallels they saw between US private universities and the Cranfield approach but it is significant that in the US such universities often include the full spread of subjects from arts through to medicine while Cranfield covers a much more limited range. It is difficult to conceive of a sufficient change in the economic and educational climate to make it possible for British universities to operate on a Cranfield basis, whether or not it would be thought desirable on other grounds.

We do not believe that the Cranfield model is necessarily appropriate to the British university system as a whole but its record of achievement in income generation is impressive and some of the principles of budgetary devolution embodied in the model might be particularly attractive to some universities. Certainly the Cranfield approach offers an antidote to the argument that in a period of financial stringency control of expenditure is necessarily best centralized. What the Cranfield approach demonstrates is that in appropriate circumstances the provision of incentives at the departmental level can make a substantial contribution to income generation, and that such an approach does not necessarily conflict with notions of strong institutional management at the centre. It suggests that universities should give greater consideration to the arguments in favour of making block grants to departments and offering incentives for departments to generate income to finance developments which cannot be funded from UGC recurrent grant.

The main message we brought back from the US however was not that any particular organizational forms were better than any other but that the management of universities in an unfriendly climate requires a much greater commitment to institutional flexibility and adaptability than was needed in the period of expansion. The US university is much more loosely organized than its British counterpart and provides opportunities for initiative at many more levels. In addition universities and their staffs are much more sensitive to the external political climate and more realistic about its impact on internal university decision-making. Finally, the US university community is more effective in identifying political decision points and using the more populist political climate to influence them. Put at its simplest, US universities have a better survival kit for the conditions of the 1980s. There are signs that British universities are responding to the changing climate. US experience suggests that new ways need to be found to influence the government's resource allocation process or universities will consistently lose out in the PESC round. Within universities, rigidities need to be removed to make the resource allocation process more flexible, less contrained by past allocations and quicker to react to external stimuli.

DECISION-MAKING MACHINERY

There are two central issues in decision-making over resource allocation. One is whether the machinery is sufficiently effective to take difficult decisions. The UGC, in its interim appraisal of the restructuring exercise, noted that universities may have exhausted their voluntary redundancies but still have further reductions to make. 'This may create,' the Chairman says, 'severe management problems in universities with their traditional form of highly democratic government.'[3] One university, Aston, has already had its difficulties made public. In September 1981 the university's Advisory Group on Budget Readjustment made a report setting out a timetable for a redundancy option. The Academic Assembly rejected it and the Council eventually deferred a decision for a year. The proposal was brought back to the Council against local and national opposition by the Association of University Teachers and was again rejected, provoking a measured editorial in the Financial Times:

'... although the reversal avoids unforeseeable legal costs, it does nothing to secure the university's future.

'The Vice-Chancellor had told the Council that voluntary departures would still leave the institution with about 30 academics too many to make ends meet. If room were also to be made to build up promising small departments, some 40 dons needed to go. But it is not only Aston's own emerging academic strengths and possibly survival that the Council has risked by bowing to the challenge of the dons' union.'[4]

At least two other universities have also been forced or been persuaded to draw back from the brink. Against this evidence the performances of Salford in creating an academic and financial plan agreed by both Senate and Council, which met the requirements of the most serious reductions in income imposed on any university, or of the University of London in embarking on a major exercise of merging and restructuring its college system, suggest that universities are by no means instrinsically incapable of taking difficult decisions. No organization facing reductions in income finds it easy to take the necessary difficult decisions, and overall the universities, in spite, and some might say because, of their machinery of government, seem so far to have acted as resolutely as most comparable institutions would have done.

The second issue is whether the machinery is adequately constructed for the problems confronting the university system. Here there is more cause for concern because the resource allocation machinery currently in place is still the product of the post-Robbins era of expansion. The people who run the machinery, both academics and administrators, have for the most part only worked in an expansionary climate. The machinery is often not well suited to the changed circumstances and peoples' attitudes do not change overnight. Chapter 5 illustrates how cumbersome and incoherent is the decision-making process in some universities, with decision points or, more properly, 'recommending powers' being dispersed so widely that decisions which should be complementary are taken in isolation one from another. It may be difficult to bring all resource allocation effectively within the remit of one body (as distinct from a finance committee having merely formal powers of decision-making over the whole field of university finance), but there seem to be few arguments, apart from past practice, to justify separating decisions about academic staffing from departmental, technical and clerical staffing and departmental expenditure generally, as we found in one university.

The machinery for the allocation of funds for equipment seemed particularly open to criticism bearing in mind the extent to which science-based departments depend on their equipment grant. It was very rare to find decisions about equipment allocations fully integrated into the rest of the machinery of academic resource allocation. Moreover, the composition of the committees, and in some cases the lack of them, seemed to indicate that the institutions concerned regarded equipment as of only second order importance in the resource allocation process.

Similarly, the links between physical and academic planning, the deployment of accommodation and minor works allocations, seemed often to be tenuous and to depend too much on overlaps of committee membership rather than on a coherent decision-making structure. Reliance on an overlapping membership can be dangerous because it assumes that committee members carry with them all the relevant considerations from one committee to the next. In fact this is rarely the case. Hard-pressed academics on committees do not necessarily make the relevant policy connections that full-time administrators assume they will do. It is only too easy for a committee member to tackle each question on its merits rather than see it as part of an overall process. It is therefore important that committee systems should explicitly reflect the linkages between different items of university business. This is particularly true in the field of resource allocation where inconsistent decision-making can both waste scarce resources and produce internal contradictions. It is equally important that universities should not underrate the damage that inefficient committee systems can cause.

Most of our systems have grown up in a decision-making climate which has almost wholly changed. If this is not recognized and systems are not adapted then universities will find it that much more difficult to cope with the pressures, external and internal, that confront them.

TIMESCALE OF DECISION-MAKING
Our examination of the cycle and timescale of Government and UGC

decision-making (Chapter 3) shows that universities need to establish a machinery which can react quickly when the recurrent grant is announced. This implies that policies and priorities need to be established in advance rather than arrived at as a result of a lengthy consideration of the actual details of the grant. The US way of concentrating committee time and internal discussion on the budgetary submission and regarding the allocation process as a more or less mechancial exercise offers an interesting comparison to British practice. British universities are inclined to be over-sympathetic to consultation — often more token than real — down an extended committee process without considering how far there is a balance of advantage in taking the necessary allocation decisions fairly quickly so that departments, academic areas and faculty boards can sort out the implications for their future planning. Again, speed may be important in obtaining the best value for money in decisions about equipment, minor works, space, maintenance and repairs.

As Chapter 5 makes clear some universities are already considering changes. But changes are hard to introduce at a time when so many other difficult decisions have to be made. We heard of one Vice-Chancellor who was able to create a small, highly centralized resource allocation committee by simply talking about it until the university at large came to believe it had been in existence all the time. But this is perhaps an isolated case of individual ingenuity. Too often, discussions about changes in committee systems become bogged down in *idées reçues* about university government which are irrelevant to the situation of the moment. On the whole the evidence suggests that changes are probably best made quickly under the pressure of external events, a financial crisis or the arrival of a new Vice-Chancellor, rather than as a result of lengthy reviews. To develop a momentum they need the active support of some of the most successful members of the academic community, who will also be the busiest, and the least tolerant of time wasting delaying tactics. Universities will need to find ways of injecting a sense of urgency into their decision-making if for no other reason than to retain their most effective members in the decision-making process.

NORMS AND FORMULAE

Nowhere does university resistance to adaptation and change show itself more clearly than in the use of norms and formulae. Almost invariably these were devised to cope with an expansionary climate; often they represented hard won compromises between subject interests. Such compromises are hard to renegotiate. Most universities use norms and formulae as an aid to rather than a determinant of decision-making, but the danger in a contracting environment, especially when new priorities are coming into view, is that the existence of such norms or formulae can reduce flexibility and be used as a defence against change. An extreme example is a university whose formula for equipment allocation preserves the ratio of costs of the purchase of equipment made when the university was first founded. This is not an argument for relinquishing any reliance on norms and formulae but for reviewing them clear-sightedly in the light of the new environment. This is easy to say but not easy to achieve. There is nothing like an argument about abstract principles of resource allocation to bring a committee grinding to a halt. Nevertheless unless these problems are tackled, or in some way by-passed, universities are in danger of remaining shackled to irrelevant criteria for resource allocation.

RESEARCH

Universities need to give more attention to the implications of their resource allocation pattern for research. On the whole they have used student numbers as the main basis for resource allocation and in a period of rapid expansion this was sensible. In a static or contracting situation other factors become important especially if research councils are to become more selective and the UGC seeks to make research expenditure a key indicator for its own resource allocation. The UGC appears to believe that the oncost of an external research grant is about 38-40% but no university in the group studied has set up a formal record of what its estimated contribution might be nor does any appear to take this into account in its resource allocation procedures. The Merrison Report calculates that 30% of the UGC recurrent grant and 66% of the equipment grant are devoted to research but none of the universities explicitly takes this into account in its allocations. As far as the equipment grant is concerned the machinery established in some universities seems almost to be devised so as not to reward research. It is hard, for example, to justify the failure of universities to take up the possibility of over-commitment in expenditure from the equipment grant. Some universities have no forum which can even begin to take an overall view of research in the institution.

ACADEMIC SERVICES AND CENTRAL ADMINISTRATION

At a technical level we have sought to identify a series of areas where there are difficulties in changing the present pattern of resource allocation but where a determined re-thinking is required. One of these is the whole area of academic services, and in particular library services where universities have for much too long allowed themselves to be guided by national data which looks on examination to be, to say the least, suspect. At the same time we must remember the librarian's dilemma that first and foremost he is expected to respond to reader demand which may be both variable and sporadic in pressure. We can allow ourselves to be sceptical about library costs because we raise sharp questions about the whole area of the central administration. A particularly critical area here is the premises budget. Early in the 1960s universities, painfully aware of the problems of administration and cost in an era of expansion, and the need for some public recognition of good management, established a series of regional

O & M units. It is an astonishing fact that the work of these units has never been referred to by universities or their administrators in our discussions with them.   Yet in the premises budget, perhaps more than any other area of the budget, there is a need for work to be undertaken on a university-wide basis to determine acceptable cost ratios, the value of alternative approaches or the mechanisms for internal costing and charging out schemes. We calculate that expenditure on university buildings ran at about £300m in 1981/82 and that the replacement cost of university buildings is now about £7,500m. The UGC expects universities will need to spend 30% more in real terms in the 1980s than in the late 1970s in adapting and modifying existing buildings. These are formidable sums. We believe universities spend less committee scrutiny time on allocations to this area of the budget than any other and yet the cost implications far outweigh those for academic items that receive the most severe scrutiny often by whole hierarchies of committees.

INTER-INSTITUTIONAL COMPARISONS

It was noticeable that the almost universal view expressed by members of staff in the universities we visited was one of general satisfaction with the systems of resource allocation in their own institutions. On the whole this represents a source of strength. There are, however, dangers in such a situation where it also indicates an unwillingness to look afresh at old problems. We have drawn attention in Chapter 6 to universities' reluctance to seek comparative data from elsewhere to guide decision-making. We believe there are far too few inter-institutional comparisons available to assist judgements about resource allocation. A particular need is to seek independent criteria for the allocation of resources in the 'Council' area of university expenditure; over this and other fields of expenditure universities have for too long made allocations on a year-to-year basis without analysing critically the trends and considering in sufficient depth alternative options. In particular we noted how little emphasis has been given by universities to monitoring the effects of resource allocation decisions. Committees are, of course, in a position to monitor changes reflected in the statistics on which they base their decisions, but in practice, once an allocation is made, the resource allocation body is much more likely to be concerned with its next problem than with any attempt to assess the effect of its last. Regular turnovers of committee membership, undertaken to bring new thinking and new faces into the system, also militate against committees having long memories. The failure to assess the effects of past decisions reflects a general unwillingness to think strategically about planning and resource allocation. If resources are going to be further reduced more radical decisions are going to be needed to be taken at the institutional level.

* * * * *

What is clear is that retrenchment and contraction demand a serious rethinking of many aspects of resource allocation. It is not just that there may be less recurrent grant and perhaps fewer students but, with a more dirigiste UGC, with a more dissatisfied public and with changing priorities within the national economy, universities are going to have to be able to make more flexible responses to external situations in quicker time than has been required in the past. Internal flexibility and the ability to move resources around within an institution are difficult for any organization, whether industrial or even military. The much publicized disagreements arising out of the 1982 Defence Review show that even in organizations arranged absolutely hierarchically, where obedience to orders makes up a significant element in the work ethic, the problems of expanding some parts while contracting others can be acute. How much more so in a university, where decisions are taken collectively and often by individuals with an interest in the result. If universities can be persuaded to view change in a more positive light such decisions will be much easier to take.

Such considerations must lead to changes in the weight we place on concepts of 'effectiveness', 'efficiency' and 'equity' in resource allocation. In the past 'equity' has been used too often to denote either incremental improvements for all departments or an equality of misery. This is not the way we have defined it in Chapter 1, nor is it the way institutions will be able to define it in the future. It will not be possible for all departments to claim that they are equally deserving of a share of new monies, nor in a contraction scenario will committees be able to evade their responsibilities by sharing out an equal cut. Criteria which include wider considerations of future institutional well-being will need to be employed. Universities will need to place more emphasis on 'efficient' systems of resource allocation, measured by whether they command institutional confidence, whether they enable decisions to be taken quickly, perhaps without the range of consultation and participation that has been traditionally required, and whether they are comprehensive and ensure that decisions are mutually consistent. Finally universities must aim for 'effectiveness' in resource allocation, ensuring that decisions are in line with more general institutional objectives and that they also give 'value for money'.

The prospects for reallocation of resources in the longer term are dependent on two factors: the ability of universities to improve their decision-making mechanisms so as to squeeze funds out of existing areas of expenditure for allocation in new areas, and success in the generation of new income. Fundamental to both is the establishment and maintenance of an effective resource allocation system which is flexible and carries the confidence of the institution. Such a system will need to be more comprehensive, based on better data, and be quicker to reach decisions than has been necessary in the past. Universities made a good start to the reallocation of resources in 1981/82 but evidence suggests that the process has only just begun.